THE INSIDER'S
GUIDE
TO ROME

THE INSIDER'S GUIDE TO ROME

NICK WYKE

ROBSON BOOKS

First published in Great Britain in 2004 by Robson Books,
The Chrysalis Building, Bramley Road, London w10 6sp

An imprint of Chrysalis Books Group

The author has made every reasonable effort to contact all copyright holders.
Any errors that may have occurred are inadvertent and anyone who for any
reason has not been contacted is invited to write to the publishers so that a full
acknowledgement may be made in subsequent editions of this work.

British Library Cataloguing in Publication Data
A catalogue record for this title is available from the British Library.

ISBN 1 86105 721 0

Typeset by SX Composing DTP, Rayleigh, Essex
Printed by Creative Print & Design (Wales), Ebbw Vale

CONTENTS

ROME ON FOOT

SHOPPING SECRETS

MUSEUMS, MONUMENTS AND GARDENS

CULTURAL ROME

RELIGIOUS ROME

ROME AFTER DARK

CHILDREN'S ROME

ACKNOWLEDGEMENTS

I would like to thank Marco, Dan and Zoe for their inspiration, patience and encouragement. They have each contributed, perhaps in ways unaware to them, to making this book possible. Thanks also to Philip Willan for his lunchtime company, and to Jennifer Lansbury at Robson Books for her meticulous and indefatigable efforts.

INTRODUCTION

While flicking through some faded newspaper cuttings from the early Nineties I noticed that a return flight from London to Rome was considered good value if it was below £300. That was more than ten years ago. Nowadays, of course, with budget airlines such as Ryanair and EasyJet flying to Rome you can touch down in the Eternal City for the price of a train fare to Manchester and still have change for a cappuccino. Never before has Rome been so accessible or popular. After the nearby hotspots of Paris, Brussels and Amsterdam, Rome is the next most visited city by UK travellers.

In the past Rome has tended to rest on its laurels. Unlike nascent post-modern cities like Bilbao and Glasgow, who vie to be European cultural capitals of the year in order to boost their profile, Rome is so culturally rich, and traditionally lethargic, that it would probably consider such a title as an onerous duty. Its age-old problem is not so much how to sell itself as how to organise itself. People the world over know that Rome is a city of beautiful stonework under the sun. What visitors have always strived for is access and mobility around the city. And now it seems they can have just that.

Since the preparations for the Holy Year 2000 celebrations kickstarted the Italian capital's 'second Renaissance' there is more to see in Rome than ever before.

Galleries, museums, churches, piazzas and fountains have shaken off the grime of centuries and been restored to their former resplendence.

For the first time in 1,500 years the Colosseum has played host to performances of classical drama – and may yet put on gladiatorial shows, minus the wild animals and grisly thumbs-down fate for Christians. Across the way the doors are open to the cavernous archaeological site of Nero's Domus Aurea (Golden House) after a lavish 25-year restoration effort.

World-class collections, some of which have been gathering dust for decades, have been revamped and reopened. For instance, at the Capitoline Museums you can now see the foundations of the most important pagan temple of ancient Rome, dedicated to Jupiter Optimus Maximus, and the pristine Palazzo Massimo alle Terme with its impressive frescoes from the Villa of Livia and its magnificent collection of Roman jewellery and coins that can be scrutinised through hi-tech magnifying equipment. At the Centrale Montemartini Museum, an offshoot of the Capitoline Museum, antique statues decorate a former power station, while, overlooking the Forum, the brand new Palatine museum showcases recently discovered mosaics. To the list can be added Villa Borghese and Palazzo Altemps, both with cutting-edge video and computer installations and multilingual audio guides to complement an A to Z of prestigious artefacts.

The Via Appia Antica breathes again thanks to a new tunnel running beneath it, where previously a ring road had spliced the Queen of ancient roads. Not since the days of Augustus have the words of the poet Propertius rung truer: 'Rome in her greatness! Stranger, look your fill!'

And for the first time since Mussolini's brutal concrete building experiments more than sixty years ago, modern public edifices by leading architects, of the sort now commonplace in Paris and London, are now firmly on the map of a city that was once entirely made from marble. There is Renzo Piano's Parco della Musica (Music Park), a striking complex of three beetle-domed concert halls built around a modern amphitheatre; Zaha Hadid's futuristic boomerang-shaped MAXXI (Museum of Art for the XXI Century); a Church of the Millennium and the sleek Museum of the Ara Pacis, both by the American Modernist Richard Meier; and a glassy new convention centre by the Italian architect Massimiliano Fuksas. In this flurry of architectural activity Rome is set to rise again. While these structures, most of which are on the periphery, gently respect the depth of the city's legacy, they also acknowledge that the country with the most mobile phones in Europe cannot live for ever in the past.

Somehow Romans have never really forgotten that their hometown was *caput mundi*, the centre of the world, two thousand years ago. Of course, their notorious *menofreghismo*, or 'couldn't-care-less' attitude, is as prevalent as the diesel in the air from the streams of scooters but, for the most part, they too have rediscovered a new pride in their city.

Two major things contributed to Rome's renewal in the 1990s. Like other cities Rome was being sacked by its own rulers: money earmarked for urban regeneration and city improvement schemes was being squandered or siphoned into the pockets of the deal brokers. Tangentopoli was an unprecedented nationwide attempt to unravel and clean up the system of kickbacks and bribery intrinsic to Italian society and politics. It is unlikely that historians will regard Tangentopoli as an unequivocal success, but to some extent it ironed out the worst excesses of Italy's bribery scandals, and money began to trickle through to worthy civic projects.

Secondly, a handsome forty-year-old mayor representing the Green Party, Francesco Rutelli, took office on the Campidoglio. Rutelli rekindled Rome's public spirit. He played a key role in encouraging the city to get real, introducing pedestrianisation and traffic regulation schemes, against which the Romans relish pitting their endless guile. As a result, by the time fifty million pilgrims arrived for the Millennial Jubilee, Rome had preened its antique good looks and, amazingly, was ready. In this century, Rutelli's do-good efforts have been continued by the current mayor Walter Veltroni.

Being progressive in a city like Rome, which until the 1990s seemed to be ensnared in civic torpor, is not an easy task for a mayor. Nowhere, at least in Europe, not even in Athens, is history so generously woven into the fabric of a city. Only recently German archaeologists discovered a sundial the size of St Peter's Square 20 metres below the modern surface of Campus Martius, the Field of Mars, in an Ancient Roman settlement bounded by the Tiber.

Rome is a confluence of history where the past inescapably impacts on the future. Nothing substantial is ever constructed here that is not delayed by archaeological finds. Even Renzo Piano's new Parco della Musica (in the Flaminio-Parioli district north of the historic centre) failed to meet its year-2000 deadline due to the discovery of important archaeological remains dating back to the sixth century BC. Typical of the city's revitalised approach to its heritage, the remains have been incorporated into the designs, giving a fascinating lesson in how a contemporary architect builds in a city so full of the past.

Justifiably famed as an open museum, walking is a manageable and unbeatable way to see Rome. The transport system, however, is simple (though it may take you a while to come to terms with the lottery that is bus numbers), cheap and relatively efficient – especially if you are coming from London. The streamlined trams are excellent. As an antidote to the often overcrowded and pickpocket-ridden bus no. 64, which oscillates between Termini Station and St Peter's, the eight-seater no. 116 bright orange electric minibus that careens around the backstreets of the centre is really quite charming.

As city centres go, it is incredibly domesticated. Safe as houses actually, not least because legions of the middle classes now inhabit the historic centre. In fact it's difficult to feel unsafe when the streets are lightly populated by a benign force of nuns, priests and monks – and the odd cardinal whisked by in a tinted-glass limousine. When in Rome, caution is best saved for crossing roads – mustering up the courage to challenge the hurtling cars and whizzing scooters. Encouragingly, Roman drivers possess the confidence and opportunism, albeit in cases bordering on bravado, that lends its own order to the perceived chaos.

Even with the mass reprinting of price lists and the inevitable rounding up of prices that followed the introduction of the euro in 2002, Rome still offers good value to northern Europeans and Americans. Genuine or 'DOC' (Denominazione d'Origine Controllata – Italian wine's seal of approval) bargains can be had in food and drink, designer clothes and gadgets, antiques and leather goods.

Finally, Rome is strikingly beautiful. Coming here in the early Nineties from the recession-hit greyness of England, in Shelley-speak, lit my soul, fired my imagination and quite literally put colour in my cheeks.

Rome's rewards are manifold. Seeing the city's golden glow on a warm summer evening; finding yourself alone in a museum in winter, face to face with an exquisite marble statue; wandering into a church and gazing in awe at a kaleidoscopic mosaic; getting high on a panorama of terracotta-tiled rooftops and sensuous domes, amid dark green pines punctuating the cityscape like exclamation marks; or simply the taste of the coffee, wine, pasta or pizza in a restaurant nestled in the corner of a medieval piazza with peeling sienna-coloured walls – they are all experiences that blow away the insipid and often pretentious substitutes that we sometimes make do with back home.

And the Romans? Well, they might appear brusque and rude at first, but until you have been on the receiving end of that primordial grunt and scowl that greets an innocent question you haven't *done* Rome. Besides, I'd rather have their genuine indifference than the overfriendly pestering advances that can be found in other countries. For the independent traveller, laissez faire usually trumps greedy interference. That's not to say locals won't be helpful. And it would be a different story altogether if you met them socially – when they are generous, well informed and frequently sardonic.

In many ways – and rather aptly as a spiritual home of Christianity – a visit to Rome can be a humbling experience, quelling the worst excesses and arrogance of tourism. Here tourists aren't special, they are just another species of a long line of invaders. You can enter a church either to look at the art or to pray, or to do both.

Rome is such a complex city that no guidebook can possibly be comprehensive, least of all one written by a single writer. This insider's guide brings you in from the outside, off the beaten track, and, by passing on some of the discoveries of my own hours of pavement-pounding, aims to offer the opposite experience of being flag-led in hordes through the Forum and fed formulaic and stodgy myths. I can't promise to eliminate the inevitable frustrations that greet the newcomer to a city that at times appears to be a law unto itself, but I can direct you towards a select few of this remarkable city's multifarious wonderful experiences.

I hope this book will steer you towards places and people that other guides relegate to footnotes and, for the length of your stay, help facilitate the illusion that you are native. Above all, my advice is: when in Rome . . . roam.

GASTRONOMIC ROME

PIZZA RUSTICA

A slice of the action

I have a well-practised ritual when travelling to Rome. The idea is to starve myself, to forsake a soggy prepacked airport sandwich and the nasty in-flight fodder in order for my appetite to be in peak condition on arrival. Then wherever I jump out in Rome I head directly to one of its many *pizza rustica* outlets and gaze in awe at the colourful mosaics of tempting toppings.

These takeaway places, also known as *pizza al taglio* (pizza by the slice), are as ubiquitous in Rome as *gelaterie*. Like many people, my entire day is punctuated with trips to the *pizza rustica* for a hearty snack. In fact, I could plot my course around the city according to which pizzas have been consumed in which piazzas.

When I first arrived in Rome and was lodging in a rundown *pensione* in the seedy area beside Stazione Termini, counting every lira until I found stable work, I lived on *pizza rustica*. What's amazing is that although that was then the tastiest, most nutritious food I could afford, it is — even with a modicum of economic stability — still a treat. How rare it is that what we most hanker after is so affordable. Now, when I'm away from Rome, pizza on the hoof is one of the things I miss most.

Rectangular slices of *pizza rustica* are sold by weight and priced according to their toppings. Toppings range from the bubbling lunar landscape of a salt-encrusted and oil-drizzled warm *pizza bianca* and its sibling *rossa* (burnished with the thinnest layer of tomato and a sprinkling of herbs), to far more elaborate and fantastical combinations.

Naturally, however, this being Italy, no food crimes are committed. There are none of the marriages in hell of the American pineapple and ham variety. Conjugal harmonies include: country sausage with broccoli; anchovies with golden courgette flowers; artichokes and cooked ham; radicchio and bubbling gorgonzola; juicy strips of wild mushrooms with spiky parsley; soft, shredded potato coated with cheese and rosemary; parma ham and olives; and wilted spinach and prawns on a layer of mayonnaise. Mayonnaise has become a popular addition to the *pizza rustica* selection.

The pizza is eaten warm, folded in two, and wrapped in paper – like ice cream, it's a perfect food to eat and amble. Or you can take away a whole medley of pizza in a box, enough for a family feast.

Excellent central takeaway *pizzerie* include Antico Forno[1] in Campo de' Fiori, Il Fornaio[2] on Via Baullari between Campo de' Fiori and Corso Vittorio Emanuele II, and another Antico Forno[3] opposite the Trevi Fountain. In Trastevere, head for Forno La Renella[4] on Via del Moro, or Sisini[5] on Via Francesco a Ripa. Zi Fenizia,[6] on Via Santa Maria del Pianto, serves delicious Kosher pizza in the Ghetto, the old Jewish quarter bounded by the Tiber, the Portico d'Ottavia, and Via Arenula.

An outstanding variation on the *pizza rustica* is devoured at the Rome-renowned Lo Zozzone[7] on a backstreet off

Piazza Navona. Its slightly sanitised new location on Via del Teatro Pace is just around the corner from its old site on Via del Governo Vecchio. Here great shields of hot *pizza bianca* are baked on the premises, sawn into pieces the size of A3 paper, hewn horizontally and filled at your request. The house speciality is rocket, bresaola and mozzarella with a dusting of paprika and parmesan and a squirt of freshly squeezed lemon juice. Other fillings include roasted Mediterranean vegetables, prosciutto, fresh figs and smoked cheese.

Opened in 1914 by the current boss's grandfather, Ugo Paladini, the original bakery became famous in the neighbourhood during World War II because the Paladini family gave away bread when food was scarce and delivered to the jails and soup kitchens. Its basement also served as a secret underground refuge. These days you'll have to pay for your pizza, but at the giveaway price of €2 a throw it costs less than a Big Mac and is infinitely more nourishing. The mineral water is also no longer gratis but, as ever in Rome, there's a fountain just around the corner.

1   ANTICO FORNO, 22 Campo de' Fiori (at the corner of Campo de' Fiori and Vicolo dei Cappellari), 06 6880 6662, open 9am–7.30pm daily, except Sun.
2   IL FORNAIO, 5–7 Via Baullari, 06 6880 3947, open 7am–8pm daily.
3   ANTICO FORNO, 8 Via delle Muratte, 06 679 2866, open 7am–9pm daily.
4   FORNO LA RENELLA, 15–16 Via del Moro, Trastevere, 06 581 7265, open 8am–9pm daily.
5   SISINI, 137 Via San Francesco a Ripa, 06 589 7110, open 9am–9pm daily, except Sun.
6   ZI FENIZIA, 64 Via Santa Maria del Pianto, 06 689 6976, open 9am–7pm Sun to Thu, 9am–3.30pm Fri.
7   LO ZOZZONE, 32 Via del Teatro Pace, 06 6880 8575, open 9am–9pm daily, except Sun.

MAGNA ROMA

A feast fit for an emperor

Just a javelin's throw from the Colosseum, where wild
beasts once feasted on the flesh of the doomed, humans can
now get a taste of Ancient Rome for themselves at a
restaurant that recreates the dining experience of the first
century AD. Or, to be more precise, authentic Roman food
of the Patricians from AD 14 to 138 – the restaurant is
named after a great period of imperial Roman history.

Professore Franco Nicastro, a bearded academic with
the large, looming presence of a gladiator, is the man behind
Magna Roma.[1] A stickler for detail, he has even created a
new profession for himself as an archaeogastronome – more
of a mouthful than a stuffed dormouse, which incidentally
isn't on the menu.

Nicastro came up with the idea while he was working
as an archaeologist unearthing kitchen pots and pans around
Rome (he still digs with a university in the city). He has
discovered and translated about a thousand ancient recipes
and, together with his staff, tested 220 of them; the
restaurant currently has fifty on the menu.

'Testing the dishes was a bit of a leap into the dark,'
says Nicastro. 'We used, let's say, the "more acceptable" ones

on the menu.' Sow's wombs, boiled flamingo and camel's hooves are among the Roman specialities that didn't find their way on to the menu, no doubt to the relief of his cooks, customers and suppliers. He explains, 'We only include a dish if we can find every ingredient. If there is just one small spice missing, we don't make it.'

This attention to detail is applied to the dining room, too, which attracts more Italians than tourists. Once you cross the threshold of Magna Roma you are transported back in time. An *ancilla*, or serving girl, wearing white robes with gold trim, greets visitors and ushers them through a Roman arch into the candle-lit room decorated with wall-to-wall frescoes.

My table is laid with terracotta bowls, modelled on those on display at Pompeii, a sharp-ended spoon and a fearsome looking knife. Neither forks nor napkins had been invented in Roman times, so staff here discreetly advise diners to use the pronged end of their spoon and the tablecloth as respective substitutes. A textbook serves as a menu. It has eighty pages and is a testimony that Nicastro takes what he calls an experiment in 'archaeological gastronomy' quite seriously. Sure, he wants to sate appetites, but he also wants diners to walk back out into the bright sunlight of the third millennium with a little knowledge from the experience.

An *aperitivo* of sweet Mulsum wine is served in earthenware cups, and a plate of *cibi sacrali* (sacred foods) includes walnuts, hazelnuts, olives, lupini beans, dates and quail eggs.

Many of the dishes are made with familiar ingredients using unfamiliar sauces, spices and presentation: cubed cuttlefish in cold-egg sauce; duck breast with turnips, leeks and vinegar; goat pate served in seashells; and pork stew cooked in cedar with honey-sweetened mushrooms. The delicious ancient lasagna, made without tomatoes which were undiscovered in classical Rome, is proof that pasta originated in Italy. 'This subtle blending of flavours that ordinarily you would never mix, and the resultant wonder of diners when they taste it, is the true secret of Roman cooking,' reveals Nicastro.

Perhaps because of its masking properties or because of the deadening effect on their palates of water piped through lead, the Romans had a keen taste for salt. A soup of peas and leeks tastes good on its own but even better with a dose of *garum* – a pungent, brownish paste made from dried herbs, leftover fish parts and salt, left to stand in the sun for a week, then mixed every day for twenty days until it becomes a liquid. Served from a glass flask, it's a bit like anchovy paste, and you only need to add a little to your plate.

Nicastro circulates among his 'students' in the role of the *magister cenae*, the official dispenser of culinary advice. Apart from the *garum* he is asked most frequently how the Romans managed to keep ice for the *nives citrata*, or lime sorbet. He explains that snow was collected from the nearby mountains during winter, compacted, wrapped in straw and stored in an underground cellar, or *nivaria*, with a sloping floor that allowed any melting water to drain away.

To further authenticate the Roman eating experience, he is happy to speak in Latin; if you're still not impressed, he can say more than just a few words in Etruscan. Though it's usually fairly morbid stuff: 'The Etruscan we speak is the language of funerals because we only know it from what was written on the tombstones that have been found.'

From a gastro-historic perspective it is a treat to eat what the emperor Hadrian and his people once ate. 'In the same way that food and drink are worshipped in Italy today, they were also an integral part of Ancient Roman life. When diners leave here they feel as though they have participated in a satisfying physical and cultural experience,' says Nicastro. In a city that on the whole tends to stick to its staples and eschews culinary invention, the restaurant has been successful in encouraging diners to try something new.

'It's not at all like the badgers' claws that are hawked in the Colosseum in *Monty Python's Life of Brian*,' says my dining companion, sucking on a hare bone. However, she expresses some reservations about the pudding, an egg custard topped with honey and sprinkled with pepper. 'It was traditionally given to young military recruits to give them strength,' explains Nicastro. One can almost hear the army cooks echoing the standard cries of mothers across the land: 'Mangia, ti fa bene!' ('Eat up, it'll do you good!')

1   MAGNA ROMA, 26 Via Capo d'Africa, 06 700 9800, open for supper Mon to Sat from April to Sept, and Tues to Sun from Oct to March, closed 2 weeks in Aug.

Reading: *The Classical Cookbook* by Andrew Dalby and Sally Grainger, British Museum Press, £8.99.
Around the Table of the Romans: Food and Feasting in Ancient Rome by Patrick Faas, Palgrave Macmillan, around £15.

^{DA}AUGUSTO

The bona fide trattoria

Every book I've ever read on Rome has a chapter in which the author raves about a family-run, home-from-home *trattoria* that he or she has frequented regularly during his or her tour of duty in the *centro storico*. Such is the ease and conviviality of eating out in Rome that it's hard not to do the same.

For me the *trattoria* Da Augusto[1] in Trastevere best captures the repasting spirit of the city. A meal there is always uncomplicated, satisfying and fun. Its effortless charm and earthiness knocks spots off the staid 'nouvelle *trattorie*' – the Italian equivalent of gastro-pubs – in trendy areas such as San Lorenzo or the sloppy food of the tourist traps.

For the uninitiated the first challenge is finding Da Augusto – lying as it does in a tiny square somewhere between Ponte Sisto and Piazza Santa Maria in Trastevere. I nearly always approach it by a different route. No meal arrived at by taxi was ever enjoyed half so much as one at Da Augusto after negotiating Trastevere's maze of back alleys on foot.

Then invariably there's a queue. This affords you time to preview what the seated are eating and stoke up the appetite. Besides, Piazza de' Renzi with its calming amber homes encircling a single tree makes a delightful outdoor waiting room – unless the wintry *tramontana* wind is whipping through the lanes. After a spell in England, being called to a table here on a warm summer's night is like the long-awaited return into the arms of a loved one.

Da Augusto is one of the last cheap *osterie* in Trastevere serving staples of Roman cuisine. A small L-shaped dining room is crammed with wooden tables and chairs and decorated with prints of Italian divas twirling forks into mounds of steaming spaghetti. (The original photos, including adorable pictures of Sophia Loren and Ingrid Bergman indulging in the 800-year-old national pastime, are housed in the Pasta Museum[2] in the tiny Piazza Scanderbeg behind the Trevi Fountain.)

The menu is extensive, but the choice limited to what is fresh and available. There are usually three choices of pasta dishes, served with rigatoni or spaghetti: a meaty ragu sauce; *all'amatriciana*, made with cured pig's cheek (*guanciale*) in a fiery tomato sauce; and *cacio e pepe*, made with the delicious, hard pecorino cheese and ground black pepper. Then, in no particular serving order, there are lentils and chick peas, wild chicory dressed with lemon and oil, and sticky potatoes baked with garlic and rosemary. Mains favour the carnivorous and include shredded beef pan-fried with *rughetta*, chicken baked *alla cacciatora* (in vinegar and herbs), and variations of meat balls and casseroles. Dessert is usually a *torta di nonna*, a cake topped with toasted pine nuts and tangy lemons that, as its name implies, looks like it's just been baked by grandma. *Vino* is red or white and the bill is scribbled on your wine-stained, grease-smudged paper tablecloth.

The food is served by a cherubic waiter and a rotating cast of nimble waitresses, usually wannabe actresses. The diners are young Romans and foreigners in the know. Those eating out at the adjacent restaurant, with its cliched chequered tablecloths and old-school waiters attired like penguins, never seem to be having half as much fun.

Augusto himself, the owner, passed away in 2002, but the *trattoria* is still infused with his wit. The restaurant's business card depicts a caricature of Augusto reproaching a customer who has complained about a hair in the minestrone. In Roman dialect he asks the startled diner: 'What do you want, a whole bloody wig?'

1   DA AUGUSTO, 15 Piazza de' Renzi, 06 580 3798, closed Sat pm and Sun.
2   MUSEO NAZIONALE DELLE PASTE ALIMENTARI, 117 Piazza Scanderbeg, 06 669 1119, www.pastainmuseum.it, open 9.30am–5.30pm daily.

❝❝ At the other end of the spectrum is Supperclub, a novel dining concept imported from Amsterdam and located in a magnificently restored palazzo between the Pantheon and Piazza Navona (at 14 Via de' Nari, 06 6880 7207, www.supperclub.nl). Eating from the so-called 'glocal' menu – basically foods sourced from all over Italy with a blip of international spin – takes place on a communal 'bed' where you are exposed to the DJ's music and light shows. In my opinion there's too much good food to concentrate on in Rome to be distracted during dining hours. Nonetheless, the room has great frescoes, the waiting staff offer free neck massages, and it's all quite innovative stuff for a city more at home with confusion than fusion!

ALBERTO PICA'S GELATERIA

Supreme ice cream

The employees of the Baroquely named Ministero di Grazia e Giustizia (Ministry of Pardon and Justice) on Via Arenula are well placed for an optimum ice-cream break. Rome's local paper often reports that panini and ice cream for the judiciary's important meetings were provided by a nearby bar – it would be an unlikely paragraph in the newspapers of less food-obsessed countries.

In a cultural piece that follows the impenetrable pages on domestic politics, the same newspaper pronounces proudly that Rome is the capital of ice cream. Evidently new ice-cream parlours are opening at an unprecedented rate in the Eternal City where each citizen eats an average of 18kg a year, nearly 10kg more than Italians who live outside the capital.

'In Rome, we've always been greedy for ice cream,' admits Alberto Pica, the owner of his renowned *gelateria*[1] and president of the Italian Ice Cream Makers Association. For the handful of passersby wandering into the knot of streets between Piazza Farnese and the Ghetto, the plants and umbrellas on the pavement outside give his shop the impression of a smart restaurant, but conceal a classic Roman bar, unadorned except for the framed 'Golden Scoop' certificates on the wall.

You might expect Pica to be fulfilling the duties of his envious post, travelling the length and breadth of the country tasting the never-ending rainbow of ice creams in Italy's 32,500 *gelaterie*. But in the morning and late evening he can be seen directing operations from the floor of his bar. In its spiritual home, he is the man who has redefined ice cream as a panacea. According to Pica it is that rare thing, a treat that manages to be healthy. Those who know how ice cream bloated Marlon Brando might disagree.

'It is not only a pleasure, but a food that can replace a meal,' he says, in between overseeing staff preparing a mountain of snacks for the ministry. Pica talks earnestly about ice cream. He is a small man of a pensionable age with hair dyed like a gameshow host. But his appetite for ice cream is without limits. Although it's hard to imagine such an elixir comes out of this cramped and prosaic space, in the course of a year the *gelateria* makes 104 flavours in the small kitchen opposite the bar.

About 28 freshly made and seasonal flavours are on offer at any one time. All the classic Italian desserts are made into ice cream including a Roman pine-nut speciality (*romano pinola*). When I visited in September they had an ice cream made from the deliciously sweet *fragolini di Nemi*, baby strawberries from the hills of the Castelli. Uniquely, there was a newly certified flavour, Manna, made from the resin of a biblical tree found in the South of Italy, which is bitter when extracted from the trunk but sweetens and solidifies after contact with the air. The finished product has a creamy, caramel taste. According to the Bible manna was 'white like coriander seed and delicious as wafers made with honey' (Exodus 16:31), and it was eaten by the Jews during their forty-year spell in the desert with Moses – though obviously not in its frozen state. 'It'll put you in a good mood,' beams Pica. 'It's organic, full of vitamins and contains only 145 calories in a typical 100g serving.'

Pica's wife sits at the cash till where she dreams up new flavours. Previously the ice-cream makers have made prosciutto and melon, gorgonzola, ginger, saffron and even shrimp flavours. But it's a seasonal thing, they tell me. At Easter they produce the traditional Neapolitan *pastiera* flavour, made with wheat berries, ricotta and candied fruit, while in June 2001 Pica created an ice cream to commemorate the sanctification of Padre Pio. It was made with eggs, almonds and, naturally, Vin Santo, a 'holy' dessert wine.

Pica gestures for me to taste the lemon ice cream, each tub made with 5kg of fruit from the Amalfi. In many *gelaterie* it is not unusual now to see 'ACE', a tangy *gusto* (flavour) made from carrot and orange and high in vitamins A, C and E. Pica has had printed four million copies of a pocket-size pamphlet about the nutritional and social properties of ice cream. According to the Roman newspaper *Il Messaggero*, youngsters are now shunning *birrerie* and fast-food joints, and making the *gelateria* the key social meeting point. This is not exactly hard news in Italy, but it contributes to the 'Renaissance' that ice-cream sellers are enjoying.

When you're wandering Rome looking for a good *gelato*, look out for a sign with a friendly looking cow, called Gelsomina, and the letter G. This means these *gelaterie* comply with the various professional bodies' high standards of hygiene, fresh ingredients and *fantasia* – imagination.

Other exceptional ice-cream pit-stops in Rome's historic centre include Della Palma,[2] a modern emporium with a cool hundred flavours; Giolitti's,[3] a traditional parlour where politicians from the nearby parliament assemble over cones and tubs to discuss the laws of the land; and Il Gelato di San Crispino,[4] not far from the Trevi Fountain, which is considered by many to serve the best ice cream in Italy – it has inventive new flavours such as meringue with hazelnuts, pink grapefruit with whisky cream, and lemon and liquorice.

1   ALBERTO PICA, 12 Via della Seggiola, 06 686 8405, open 8am–2am daily, except Sun.
2   DELLA PALMA, 20/23 Via della Maddalena, 06 6880 6752, open 8am–1.30am daily.
3   GIOLITTI, 40 Via degli Uffici del Vicario, 06 699 1243, open 7am–10pm daily.
4   IL GELATO DI SAN CRISPINO, 42 Via della Paneterria, 06 679 3924, open noon–12.30am daily except Tues, and till 1.30am Fri & Sat.

DIANE SEED'S ROMAN KITCHEN

Food fresh from the market

What could be a more civilised start to a cookery course in Rome than dinner at the former home of one of Rome's most aristocratic families, the Doria Pamphilj (see the 'Galleria Doria Pamphilj' chapter, page 119)? There are 140 apartments in the rambling Palazzo Doria Pamphilj, which skirts, on two fronts, Via del Corso and Piazza Venezia. Through the ages scores of foreigners in Rome have been fortunate enough to find accommodation here at a very favourable rate, thanks to the magnanimous nature of the late princess and her English husband.

Two of the apartments are occupied by Diane Seed, a Londoner who came to Rome when she fell in love with an Italian man in 1970. She lives in one apartment and runs a cookery course[1] in the other. Over thirty years, as Italian food fads came and went and came again in England, Seed has become something of an authority, even among Italians, on its native cuisine.

The five-day cookery course (Monday to Friday) begins with a Sunday evening welcome dinner hosted in the vast living room of Seed's apartment, with its mock

Corinthian columns, groaning bookshelves and tall windows overlooking Piazza Venezia, traditionally one of Rome's focal points of public assembly. Seed recalls her surprise when, in the 1970s, she looked up from her reading and saw for the first time a sea of red flags breezing past her first-floor window during a Communist protest march: 'It was like a scene from *Dr Zhivago*.'

The welcome meal is an ice-breaking taster of foods from different regions. For antipasto there's a specially delivered *burrata*, a creamy hulk of brilliant white cheese, from Puglia; a platter of bresaola, from the mountains around Bergamo, alongside its favourite companion, rocket; and a *mozzarella di bufala* from the plains of Campania, the size of a matronly bosom and cut liberally into large chunks. One of the guests reports that Jamie Oliver's preferred method is to tear the mozzarella, to which Seed responds: 'That's disgusting. It shows a lack of respect for the fabric of the cheese.'

The *primo piatto* is a home-made pesto, traditionally from Liguria and made minutes before serving to retain the basil's freshness. Instantly, the aroma of the basil and garlic fills the room as it mixes with the deliberately crunchy (*al dente*) linguine. There's no standing on ceremony dining with Seed. 'Tuck in,' she says, 'Pasta waits for no one.' It is to become a familiar cry throughout the course.

To follow, we had green beans and a hunk of veal cooked in milk, which broke into tender pink flakes. We rounded off the meal with a large bowl of white and black grapes – though I missed coffee and dessert as James Taylor was giving a free concert at the other end of Via del Corso in Piazza del Popolo. Not even in Rome can you have your cake and eat it.

You could say, where Seed is concerned, that all foods lead to Rome. She cooks relatively simple dishes with the freshest seasonal ingredients, which, in a nutshell, is the 'secret' of Italian cooking. She says, 'Year round we have tremendously good produce delivered to our markets. Because of the demands of the capital it's even better quality here than, say, in Puglia, and there's more variety.'

On her own Seed usually drives to the market in the centre of the former blue-collar Testaccio district, but with a group in tow (Diane's seedlings, as I came to think of us), on the third day of the course, we stroll a few blocks to Campo de' Fiori and Rome's most picturesque daily market. Here, tumbling rubicund and caramel buildings are wedged together around the oblong piazza, with triple-glazed windows and their coats of paint cracked like sunburn.

Farm workers in three-wheeled vans bring in demi-johns of coarse unadulterated wine, eggs still stuck with straw, and newly unearthed vegetables that look like weeds – wild borage, chicory, sorrel, dandelion and rocket. Lucky dips of mixed wild salad leaves (*misticanza*) can be found at some stalls. In the best Italian family tradition, grandmothers perch on stools shucking peas into their laps. Over the years Seed has picked up many tips and recipes from market stallholders, who hawk their produce with flattering cries of persuasion and stuff housewives' bags *in abbondanza*.

The market's palettes change daily, and Seed confesses, 'I have never lost the sense of wonder and excitement at the beginning of every season as the fresh new produce appears in the local markets.'

In fact, you could chart any season's arrival from the fresh produce at any one of Rome's outdoor markets. By the time Easter comes oranges have been supplanted by dark strawberries from Terracina, and the stalls are piled with bunches of asparagus wrapped like dynamite, floppy green beans *(fave)* to be eaten raw with salty pecorino cheese, and sweet baby tomatoes, still on their vine stalks, that seem related to the almost black velvety cherries from the Adriatic coast that begin to appear about now. Then from out of nowhere mandarins stage a comeback, hand-picked and still dressed in their leaves. Small golden apricots, honeydew melons with patterned skins like china, and peaches the size of babies' bottoms soon follow. It is a sensory experience that shames an English fruit and veg market with its perennially bland imports. But then, England is not blessed with the sun.

It's a close call but, of all the seasons, Seed most keenly anticipates the *bei ottobrini romani* (Rome's beautiful October days) that deliver shiny chestnuts, silky *funghi porcini*, artichokes, cardoons and pumpkins – all wonderful ingredients for soup and pasta at the onset of winter.

With a hawk-like studiousness, Seed acquires fennel, artichokes and courgette flowers (*fiori di zucchini*) that look like amber snapdragons. We pick up some veal for the saltimbocca at Antica Norcineria Viola,[2] a *salumeria* established in 1890 on the Campo. Its display counter looks like the meat pages of a how-to-cook tome, and purchases are wrapped in a delicate mauve bag. 'It's not every day that pigs' trotters get dressed up like lingerie,' jokes Seed.

Before we leave the market, we grab a cappuccino and a slice of plainly salted *pizza bianca* hot out of the oven from Antico Forno at the corner of Campo de' Fiori and Vicolo dei Cappellari (see page 4 in the 'Pizza Rustica' chapter). Next door you can watch the bakers at work.

The shopping excursion serves as inspiration for the rest of the week's cooking. Back at Seed's lofty turquoise Roman kitchen a typical cooking day starts at a considerate 10.30am. Everyone mucks in making four or five dishes. By midday the first bottle of wine is opened; and we eat our creations during a gently paced lunch. The day's work finishes shortly after 2pm when we wander home for a siesta, perhaps squeeze in a visit to a museum and then meet again to eat out in the evening (which isn't part of the course).

I'm gathered with a handful of amateur cooks from America and Australia – apparently Seed is big in the former and very big in the latter – and another Englishman, Peter, who's in 'soft retirement', taking a delayed gap year with his wife who is around the corner at the Gregorian university learning Italian with a classful of nuns. Our common bond is a passion for Italian cuisine.

First we make *saltimbocca alla romana*, veal with wafer-thin slices of dry-cured ham briefly fried in butter and wine. The hidden sage leaves, skewered by a toothpick, are said to make the meat 'jump in the mouth'. Next we prepare another local classic, *carciofi alla romana* (artichokes Roman style). The plant-like vegetable heads are slowly stewed in a stock of mint, garlic and wine, rather than fried *alla giudia*, or Jewish style. We also stuff each of the courgette flowers with anchovies and batons of mozzarella, before they are twirled in batter and shallow fried.

Seed's food tips are in the best Italian tradition: they are non-scientific, of the sort passed down by peasants and fishermen. For example, she pops a cork in the water with the octopus to tenderise it and swills the basil in cold water rather than running a potentially damaging flow of water over the leaves.

She peppers the practicals with Roman tales about love, traffic and bureaucracy, and plenty of cooking stories and reflections on the Italian character of which Italian men seem to bear the brunt.

There are also jibes at her next-door neighbour, Prime Minister Silvio Berlusconi, whose bodyguards mistakenly arrested a friend of Seed's staying at a nearby *pensione* after she'd taken some photos from her balcony – they suspected she might be a terrorist sizing up an attack.

According to Seed it is her academic curiosity and Englishness that have helped her towards a heightened understanding of Italian cuisine. Her impartial overview of the regions gives her a more complete understanding of the country's *cucina* than many of its own cooks. 'I wasn't born in Italy, so I'm not confined to one region. This has enabled me to remain neutral in my explorations and writings about Italian food.'

And if Seed constantly bangs the drum of unfussy simplicity in the kitchen, this too has been her recipe for success in publishing. Her simply titled debut *The Top One Hundred Pasta Sauces*, published by Ten Speed Press, has sold more than one million copies worldwide, and must have sated countless more appetites. The Italian Tourist Board must owe her an honorary award.

1   DIANE SEED's ROMAN KITCHEN, 112 Via del Plebiscito, 06 679 7103, www.italiangourmet.com. Week-long courses run throughout the year. (For a three-day cookery course with Signora Gabriela Pisani, at her B&B on the Janiculum hill, see page 244 in the 'Bed & Breakfast' chapter.)

2   ANTICA NORCINERIA VIOLA, 42 Campo de' Fiori, 06 6880 6114, closed Sun.

" At my local market in Trastevere's Piazza San Cosimato I can never escape the fish lady with a scarf wrapped round her head. She hosts a little stall by the fountain twice a week. If I catch her eye, she hooks me with her smile, addresses me as *dottore* (because of my glasses, I think) and holds up a fish by its tail, its scales mirroring the sun. Her helper slices open the fish and deftly removes its guts over a bucket of water. She wraps it up like a gift with a bunch of parsley and recites a simple recipe as a doctor does a prescription. '*Buon appetito*,' she says, stuffing my lunch into my rucksack with a wink.

CAFFÈ

The aroma di Roma

You'll be served a pretty good coffee in most bars in Rome. But there are, according to the Romans, two sacred citadels to the coffee bean situated within roasting distance of each other either side of the Pantheon. The older establishment is Caffè Sant'Eustachio[1] on the site of a bar since the 1800s and wearing its present look since 1938. At peak times its bar gets several people deep. How it makes its coffee is shrouded in secrecy; there's even a shield around the roasting machine. What we are told is that 100 per cent arabica coffee beans are slowly wood roasted. The owner has a collection of about 200 old coffee makers that he hopes one day will form the basis for a coffee museum. The speciality here is *gran caffè* – a creamy, frothed-up double espresso already sweetened.

The Tazza d'Oro[2] across the way is principally a *torrefazione del caffè* or a coffee roasting house – the only one with a licence in the *centro storico*. According to its owner, the higher quality the beans the less caffeine – here there is about 0.7 to 0.9 per cent per serving. Romans come from all over the city for its *granita di caffè* – a shot of coffee and crushed ice topped with whipped cream.

But my favourite place for coffee is Bar San Calisto,[3] in the picturesque district of Trastevere and just around the corner from the main square, Piazza Santa Maria in Trastevere. Set in an unremarkable, misshapen piazza that becomes an overcrowded car park in the evenings, the bar is nothing fancy. It has not changed its décor in years; tobacco-stained walls are hung with fading pictures of prize fighters. The *barista* behind the shiny chrome bar is dressed in a burgundy 1950s waiter's jacket, usually with a tea towel slung over his shoulder.

Marcello, the owner for 32 years, is a short, barrel-chested man from the Abruzzo, with a boyish smile. He sits placidly at the till by the door where he tots up customers' bills. If pushed he will tell you how the young Isabella Rossellini used to come to the bar for breakfast each morning and he'll point to the Muhammad Ali memorabilia on the wall that she sent him as a gift from New York. But there's no fawning here. All customers are treated the same.

Marcello's philosophy is simple and quite refreshing: low prices and good, simple products. In most places in Italy customers are charged double to consume food or drink *al fresco*, and in some of the tourist hotspots around the Pantheon and Piazza Navona where a cappuccino commands €10, the system is virtually a licence to print money. But at Marcello's bar, the prices are the same whether you stand up inside or sit down outside (the only two options as there is not really any indoor seating). When I first moved to Rome, on winter mornings it was warmer to sit outside the bar in the sunshine than in my unheated flat.

Drinks and ice cream are available here, but no tourist frills such as postcards for sale. The beer and spirits are cheaper than if you bought them in a supermarket in England, and the chocolate ice cream that comes out of silver churns built into the bar is made from Marcello's own special recipe.

There was a time when the bar was a magnet to junkies and it has been closed down on more than one occasion. But over the years it has developed a shabby-cool reputation, partly from its appearance in the hi-tech Tiscali adverts.

Customers seem to come in two distinct waves. In the morning it is a neighbourhood bar for local families who sit bemoaning the demise of local shops and the influx of foreigners. Come sundown the clientele changes. There's a vibrant Bohemian crowd of students, artists and expats. You will be guaranteed to share your *caffè corretto* (coffee 'corrected' with a spirit, in this case grappa) with some varied company, and much of it Roman.

1   CAFFÈ SANT'EUSTACHIO, 82 Piazza Sant'Eustachio, 06 6880 2048, open 8.30am–1am daily.
2   TAZZA D'ORO, 84 Via degli Orfani, 06 678 9792, open 8am–8pm Mon to Sat.
3   BAR SAN CALISTO, Piazza San Calisto, Trastevere, 06 589 5678, open 5.30am–2am Mon to Sat.

BABINGTON'S TEA ROOMS

Tea for the Grand Tourists

Fine coffee can, of course, be found on nearly every street corner in Rome. A good brew of tea *all'inglese* – the Italians consider the English to be the world's chief tea drinkers and connoisseurs – is harder to find. The best tea in Roman bars is iced: a fragrant, home-made peach or lemon tea that is served from old wine or water bottles. It is highly recommended on exhausting jaunts around town on summer days.

But for those who can't do without a cuppa – and I don't mean of the hotel flask and powdered milk variety – a refuge is on hand. A century before the faux-Irish assembly-kit pubs sprang up like weeds across Rome, the city had another sort of home-from-home watering hole.

In 1893 Babington's Tea Rooms[1] began serving freshly made tea and cake to weary Anglo-Saxon tourists. On their opening, the English language newspaper, the *Roman Herald* reported: 'A long-felt want in Rome has at last been supplied, and that is a tea room where ladies or gentlemen, hard at work sightseeing . . . could go to refresh themselves with a comforting cup of tea or coffee, with the necessary adjuncts.'

Situated at the foot of the Spanish Steps, in a location that would turn Ronald McDonald green with envy, the tea rooms were founded by two intrepid young Englishwomen who had traded London for Rome with £100 capital to start a business.

When Misses Babington and Cargill first put the kettle on at their tea rooms, Piazza di Spagna was at the heart of Rome's English Quarter – there were already a chemist, a bank, a church, a bookshop and lodgings in the vicinity catering for the needs of English travellers and residents. As far back as the 1740s an inn in the piazza had changed its name from Lo Scudo di Francia to La Villa di Londra in order to attract wealthy British tourists; a branch of Barclays bank followed; and in 1771 a Mrs Millar was grateful to find 'three or four homely dishes . . . such as bacon and cabbage, boiled mutton and bread puddings' on the menu at Albergo Pio.

In the eighteenth century, if young Henry and Henrietta were not the most cultured specimens of their age and the thought of outing them into London society made their parents cringe, a common solution was to pack them off on a Grand Tour – Richard Lassels was the first to use the term in 1670, in the preface to his book of travel tips, *A Voyage to Italy*. For a gap year or several, between Paris and Naples, they were free to purge themselves of boorishness and soak up a bit of culture with a capital C.

In the days before the Orient Express first pulled out of Victoria bound for Venice, the journey across the Alps by horse and carriage was long and dangerous. Fortunately for the privileged tourists, they were often accompanied by an entourage of hardy servants and classically educated tutors, and carried letters of reference and introduction to the ambassadors and aristocratic families of the courts of Europe.

Rome was the Tour's ultimate finishing school. It was also its most southerly port of call before excavations began at Herculaneum in 1738 and Pompeii in 1748. Henry James described arriving in Rome in a letter to a friend in 1869: 'At last – for the first time – I live! It beats everything: it leaves the Rome of your fancy – your education – nowhere. It makes Venice – Florence – Oxford – London – seem like cities of pasteboard . . . for the first time I know what the picturesque is' (from *The Letters of Henry James*, Vol. 1, 1843-75). The Eternal City had its ruins and antiquities, its Papal offerings and Renaissance splendours – much of the art still in situ and fresh with original colour. It also had courtesans, good food and wine, gaming and the sun shone endlessly. The whole package offered an unprecedented sense of freedom for the beef-fed offspring of the nobility fresh out of England's public schools.

In fact, in a city that was then no bigger than a market town, its ruins and salons must have been cooing with lords and ladies. Before the eighteenth century people had only taken to the road in order to hunt, study, explore, make a pilgrimage or fight a war – but the tourists enjoyed bartering for antiques, having their portraits painted standing in front of the Colosseum or the Pantheon, and pondering and sketching the ancient ruins.

Today's tourists continue these traditional pastimes around Piazza di Spagna where, in the best Italian keep-it-in-the-family tradition, Babington's Tea Rooms have remained in the Cargill family since their opening. The current manager, Rory Bruce, is a descendant of the pioneering Miss Cargill. And it looks set to stay that way. 'Because of its desirable location we've had many approaches to take over the premises, but it's the last of its sort in Rome,' says Bruce, who shares the running of the tea rooms with his cousin.

Not even World War II could drive the Cargills out of the tea business as something akin to the spirit of the Blitz was kept simmering in this slice of England in Rome. The rooms continued to serve tea during the entire nine months of the German occupation of Rome. The closed sign was hung up just once for a few hours when shrapnel smashed the windows on the day the Germans marched in.

Today the frenzied activity in the Piazza, the streets thronging with shoppers and the Steps draped with Rome's youth and tourists, contrasts with the home-hearth peace of Babington's. Although the scene filmed here for *The Talented Mr Ripley* suggested it, there are no continental-style outdoor tables. Once inside you are transported to the relative quiet of small-town England. Cups and saucers are neatly laid out on raffia mats, and ruched, patterned curtains dress lead-latticed windows. The orderly seating is a world apart from the stand-up anarchy of a Roman coffee bar. At about €10 a pot the prices are on a par with a plush hotel.

The fireplace is lit for a couple of months a year and must offer a homely respite from a day's shopping during the winter sales. Around this time a date for the diary of all expats is Babington's traditional Christmas carol concert. The tea rooms are also host to small recitals of classical music organised in association with Rome's leading music venues.

According to Bruce, though, this is a cosy tea shop with a difference. Not only do the tea rooms have an all-female staff – traditionally in Italy waiting staff in both restaurants and bars are male – it doubles as a sanctuary from the paparazzi. 'Politicians and film stars know they can come here without being bothered by fans or the media,' says Bruce, who also reveals that sterling fashionistas have been lately taking their lapsang souchong on the premises. Amid the gentle chink of china the stars can browse the English papers while nibbling neat home-made cakes of the sort you might find at a village fair.

Thirty-five blends of tea lead the quaint menu, including Celestial Jasmine, Flowery Orange Pekoe, Pinhead Gunpowder (a pungent green tea rolled into balls) and Babington's Royal, dedicated to Queen Elizabeth II on her Jubilee Year visit to Rome, in October 2000. Edible accompaniments include high-tea treats such as Welsh rarebit, hot buttered crumpets and home-made truffle ice cream.

Of course a visit to Babington's goes against the 'When in Rome . . .' ethos, but the tea rooms seem to have earned their place in Rome's cultural fabric. There is also affordable Italian wine on the menu, and that's something you won't find at Mrs Miggins's back home.

1   BABINGTON'S TEA ROOMS, 23 Piazza di Spagna, 06 678 6027, open 9am–8pm daily.

Reading: *In Ruins* by Christopher Woodward, Vintage, £7.99.

❝ If you visit the Roman Forum today with one of the many guides on hand, you will be able to piece together a mental image of Rome in its majestic splendour. The Grand Tourists, however, had a far more enriching experience according to Christopher Woodward in his book *In Ruins*:

In their minds they saw not only the actuality of a past civilisation but also London, the future, and the hopes

and frailties of their own lives. Ruins were oppor-
tunities to imagine — to imagine, to moralise, to
dream, and to contemplate mortality and regeneration, as well as the eternal contest between man and
Nature. Today we learn more, but we feel less.

To deepen their appreciation of art, the well-
connected would accept invitations to admire the
private collections of Rome's wealthy families such as
the Albani, Chigi, Farnese and Ludovisi to name but a
few. Picnics in the parks of their hosts' villas were
popular, and when it rained or was too hot they
would perambulate the cool interior of St Peter's.
According to their journals and etchings of the time
many of the young visitors were equally captivated by
the fireworks displays at the Castel Sant'Angelo when
five thousand rockets were fired into the sky from a
giant spinning wheel.

In an age free from today's rigid art trafficking laws
the Grand Tourists would, occasionally, bag an
authentic objet d'art. Nothing was shifted on the scale
of the Elgin Marbles, but by the end of the eighteenth
century a traveller and collector of antiquities,
Edward Clarke, declared that Rome was 'exhausted of
every valuable relic'.

More often than not, however, tourists would visit
workshops where a contemporary artist could
reproduce a range of 2,000-year-old Roman
sculptures, which were themselves copies of Greek
originals. Etchings, too, were popular mementoes,
especially those by Piranesi, as were fans painted with
views of the city. And pen-and-ink caricatures of the

Brits abroad by local artists illustrated the beginnings of a love-hate relationship, or a sort of parallel snobbism, between the visitors and the visited that still thrives today, not only in Italy.

The English were mocked as the only nation whose women would traipse around the pastoral ruins of the Forum in the scorching daytime heat dressed in heavy gowns. (Today, however, fur-clad Romans sneer at under-dressed tourists in shorts and football shirts in the middle of winter, even though it may be touching 70°F (21°C).) In turn, many of the English Grand Tourists were ignorant and contemptuous of the Italian way of life. Even the great liberal, Shelley remarked that 'countesses smell so of garlic that an ordinary Englishman cannot approach them.'

The Grand Tourists spent a great deal of money abroad and due to these expenditures outside of England some English politicians were very much against the institution of the Grand Tour. Samuel Johnson considered time spent among ruins as a suspension of time, arguably a delaying tactic for the nobs from facing their responsibilities back home. Woodward agrees: 'Ruins are a gentle riposte to the relentless march of progress, and the precious hours we spend among them a temporary dislocation of the forward, linear momentum which dominates so much of our lives.'

To service this elite of travellers, maps and guidebooks began to appear and the tourist industry came into being. The Grand Tour also made an important contribution to British neoclassical architecture in the Georgian period, as the British sought to recreate Rome's imperial grandeur in their own backyards. In the garden of his house in Ealing, Pitshanger Manor, the architect John Soane created a fragmentary temple under brambles and ivy and invited his guests to reconstruct its Roman magnificence as an erudite parlour game.

The French Revolution of 1789 marked an abrupt end to the Grand Tour proper – no one wanted to risk having their (blue) blood spilled in the name of culture. But travellers had caught the Rome bug and by the early nineteenth century, when the railways were poised to change the face of travel across the continent forever, British visitors were already so numerous in Rome that hoteliers referred to all tourists as 'English'. At a ceremony at the Sistine Chapel in 1817 the German writer Stendhal noted, in *A Roman Journal (1827-29)*, that out of 200 female spectators, 195 were English. 'I am indeed making an English Journey,' he grumbled, 'without ever setting foot beyond the bounds of Italy.'

LAZIO'S WINE RENAISSANCE

The pick of the enoteche

When I lived in Trastevere I used to pick up a litre and a half of wine in a plain bottle from one of the market stallholders in Piazza San Cosimato, taking back the empty for a refill twice a week. The wine was a hazy leonine gold, drinkable but, in retrospect, a bit rough. Arguably, the seductive connection between wine and place, particularly when on holiday in sunny climes, stretches the limits of taste – and I think this was the case with my market wine supply. However, I liked the idea that it had been brought into the centre of town from the countryside where all the mud-caked verdant bounty of the market stall had been harvested. It made me think 'organic', though I probably wouldn't have used that word when I moved to Rome in the early 1990s.

Chances are it was unfiltered and made from the most recent vintage – most wines are drunk young in Italy. The wine guru Hugh Johnson, a founder member of Rome's Wine Academy, wrote in his classic *Story of Wine*:[1] 'The important thing is to experience the flavour of a place in what we drink.' And the best wines I'd ever tasted here, or so it seemed then, had always been made in an allotment, not a winery.

Four hundred years ago Romans didn't have to rely on country folk to deliver wine to the city. The gentle inclines of Via Veneto and the Pariolo district were blanketed in vines, many flourishing until the late nineteenth century. The last substantial vine in central Rome is now in the service-entrance courtyard of the Grand Hotel. It seems as old as the city itself and is of an unknown grape variety. The hotel staff resolutely makes a case of wine from it each year.

Now, a local wine in Rome usually means from the Castelli Romani hills about 25km (15 miles) southeast of the city. If you fly into Rome's Ciampino airport you get a good overview of the shimmering vineyards that coat the lower slopes of the Castelli. It makes a pleasant drive to turn off the A2 *autostrada* at Monte Porzio Catone, where many of the Frascati producers are based, and then follow the wine roads past the volcanic lakes of the Colli Albani hills to Velletri.

With the exception of Frascati, wines from Lazio are little known outside of the region. In many Roman *trattorie* there is no second menu with an encyclopaedic list of globally sourced wines. Instead a carafe of red or white in quantities of un *quarto*, *mezzo* or *litro* will be plonked on the table. This kind of wine drinking is inexpensive, but pot luck. If you have a refined palate, brace yourself. But be prepared to be surprised, too. The wine may not even be Roman at all – barrelled wines from Sardinia or Sicily are common in Roman kitchens. Whatever its provenance it is likely to be cold, dry and not especially strong. Even weaker when cut with mineral water, a common Italian habit.

Of course, for Lazio it's hard to beat off regional rivals such as Tuscany and Piedmont with their ornate and robust reds, and Veneto's slick array of whites and lighter reds, plus a whole host of hotshot wines emerging from Sicily and Puglia. But despite the competition, Lazio's wine industry has improved by leaps and bounds, and now it seems Lazio has finally bid *arrivederci* to the worst of its bread-and-beans peasant wines. Recognition of progress came when the Fontana Candida group picked up a gold medal in the 'price quality' category at a recent wine awards in Rome for its Frascati Superiore Santa Teresa 2000 ('superiore' means it has 0.5 per cent more alcohol). After a slump in Frascati's quality and reputation, producers considered this to be a breakthrough.

The rebirth of wine in Lazio has been accompanied by a wine bar boom in Rome. These revamped *enoteche* are more sophisticated than the *osterie* of old. However, among the vast selection of northern wines on their shelves it's not always easy to find a wine from Lazio. According to Philip Dallas, the author of *Italian Wines*,[2] the finest wines of Rome come from the estate of Prince Boncompagni Ludovisi, just past Ciampino airport and known as Fiorano. The two whites are made from straight malvasia – the most common grape in Lazio along with trebbiano – and semillon, and the red is a merlot-cabernet. Sadly, however, Fiorano wines are almost unobtainable.

Other wines to look out for are Cantina Cerquetta's Antico Cenacolo Frascati Superiore (their motto is 'Nunc est Bibendum' – 'The time has come to drink'), and Paola di Mauro's ruby red Vigna del Vassallo from the Marino zone. The owner of the exclusive Hassler Hotel personally recommends Riccardo Cotarella's Montiano from Falesco, made from 100 per cent merlot grapes.

For the best in Roman wines, Trimani[3] wine stores
has a superlative stock of Italian wines arranged by region
and a window display featuring premier local bottles. Its
adjacent wine bar offers affordable lunches to queue for and
evening wine-tasting courses.

No musings on Lazio's wines would be complete
without a mention of its most unusually named tipple, Est!
Est!! Est!!! In 1110, Bishop Johann Fugger, a devout oeno-
phile, travelling from Augsburg to Rome, sent a servant ahead
of him to chalk up 'Est!' ('It is' in Latin) on the doors of *osterie*
with quaffable wine along the route. The servant was so
impressed by the wine in Montefiascone, a town north of
Rome on the shore of Lake Bolsena, he wrote out the
accolade three times with exclamation marks to boot. Bishop
Fugger agreed with his recommendation and stayed in the
town drinking Montefiascone wine for the rest of his life.

I imagine it would be most helpful for visitors –
though undoubtedly open to abuse – if a similar system was
adopted in Rome's drinking holes. Here, then, is a handful
of Roman wine bars to merit the historic three 'Ests'.

Cavour 313[4] is a charming, cosy place with more than
500 varieties of wine in its cellar, a youngish crowd and
delicious *torta rustica*, a heightened version of quiche.
Bevitoria Navona[5] near Piazza Navona has its cellars among
the ruins of Domitian's theatre; Cul de Sac[6] offers a VIP
viewing of the 'talking' statue Pasquino (see page 70 in the
'Marble Oracles' chapter); and Enoteca Ferrara[7] in
Trastevere serves wholesome organic food along with its
wine, in a candlelit back garden when the weather is warm.

Enoteca Corsi[8] was originally a *vini ed oli* shop where
locals came to replenish bottles of wine and olive oil. Then
the owners began serving a plate of pasta with a glass of wine

to the men delivering barrels from the Castelli hills. News soon spread on the neighbourhood grapevine that the food was as good as the wines, and a few tables were put out for locals. Demand burgeoned and eventually the larger adjacent room was opened as a family-run restaurant, where today an army of aunts serves delicious food with benign efficiency from an antique glass and wood display cabinet.

On weekday lunchtimes the ample main room bustles with Italian office workers seated beneath the bright halo-tube lightbulbs. The walls are posted with glowing reviews and colourful wine maps of the different regions of Italy. Roman specialities include *stracciatella* soup (chicken broth with parmesan and whisked egg), *gnocchi* on Thursdays, *baccala* (fried salt cod fillets) on Fridays and roasted *abbacchio* (milk-fed lamb). You can almost taste the family pride in the dishes. As you would expect with the equivalent of a Roman off licence next door, there's a wide choice of wine on tap to accompany the simple *trattoria* fare.

In fact the family even has its own crest of arms on the napkins: 'Finché vieni da Corsi . . . non avrai rimorsi' (literally, 'As long as you come to Corsi, you won't have any regrets'). And if you're looking for a memorable meal without fiddly food, stuffy staff or deluxe prices, you certainly won't 'regret' a visit.

1   *Hugh Johnson's Story of Wine* by Hugh Johnson, Mitchell Beazley.
2   *Italian Wines* by Philip Dallas, Faber & Faber.
3   TRIMANI, 37b Via Cernaia, 06 446 9630, open 11.30am—12.30am Mon to Sat.
4   CAVOUR 313, 313 Via Cavour, 06 678 5496, open 12.30pm—2.30pm & 7.30pm—12.30am Mon to Sat, 7.30pm—12.30am Sun.
5   BEVITORIA NAVONA, 72 Piazza Navona, 06 6880 1022, open 11am—1am daily.

6   CUL DE SAC, 73 Piazza Pasquino, 06 6880 1094, open
    12.30pm–3.30pm & 7pm–12.30am daily.
7   ENOTECA FERRARA, 1a Via del Moro, 41 Piazza Trilussa, 06 5833
    3920, open 10am–3pm & 6pm–12.30am Mon to Sat,
    6pm–12.30am Sun.
8   ENOTECA CORSI, Via del Gesù 88, 06 679 0821, open noon–8pm
    Mon to Sat.

INTERNATIONAL WINE ACADEMY OF ROMA

Mastering the art of wine tasting

At Rome's gleaming new International Wine Academy of Roma[1] some workmen are applying finishing touches to the upstairs rooms. They are slapping on coats of paint over a beautiful aqueous fresco that borders the ceiling. I am horrified. I consider calling the Ministry of Culture and Fine Arts on the spot. 'Don't worry,' my host, Valentina Morriconi, director of the academy, reassures me, 'they're not real.' It turns out that the frescoes were not 400 but four years old. And painted not by Michelangelo, but by the design crew of the film director Bernardo Bertolucci for his film *Besieged* (1998).

I thought the Wine Academy looked familiar. I recalled the actor David Thewlis looping down the fine wrought-iron staircase, and playing his piano to Thandie Newton with the open shutters framing a view of flowers cascading down the Spanish Steps. In such a conspicuous location – it's the first *palazzetto* on your left as you come out from the Piazza di Spagna metro station – the academy should generate a great deal of its own publicity. Inside there's a newly furnished air to the place that will mellow with age, and its plush tasting rooms and leafy terrace incline even the least bibulous to get serious about wine.

The Romans have been drinking wine for at least two thousand years – they were passed the flagon, so to speak, by their forebears, the Etruscans – so a half-day or three-day wine course in the centre of Rome feels like wine at the root of its tradition. And as the world's biggest producer, there's a lot to digest about Italian wine.

Wine expert Andrea Sturniolo takes his students through the fundamentals of wine tasting and a potted history of Italy's wine regions. 'When you sniff a wine if it is good the mouth will start to water,' he says, urging us to 'use the wine as a mouthwash.'

It's interesting, given Britons' unquestioning faith in Italian food and drink, to learn that in the past fifteen years the Italian wine industry has been working hard to shed its image as an exporter of fairly neutral, all-rounder food wines. Sturniolo grimaces when he reads a bottle's label that claims its contents complement fish, meat, pasta or can be enjoyed on its own. 'It is just too general,' he says, 'wine is much more subtle than that.'

Born in Turin of Sicilian parents and having been the sommelier to Giorgio Locatelli at Zafferano's restaurant in London – 'the real crucible of international wine, because they import from all over the world' – Sturniolo under-stands contemporary wine. But by Italian standards he is a relative latecomer to the joys of wine. It wasn't until he left home, aged seventeen, to do his national service in the air force, that he first tasted decent wine. Until then he had only sneaked mouthfuls from a screwcap flagon that his father kept for months on end beside the cooker. '*Che schifo*' ('How disgusting'), he says, screwing up his face as though the sour taste still haunts his palate.

Thankfully the days of literally blinding wines are over, and Sturniolo feels Italy is enjoying a wine renaissance, with Tuscany leading the way: 'Modern Italian wines are generally more pleasant. They possess fuller aromas and flavours, are cleaner and oakier.'

Like its food, Italian wines have strong regional attachments. Sturniolo believes a wine should be true to its background, and relishes being able to associate the taste of a wine with its region's history and culture. He says, in an apt analogy for a wine school overlooking the designer-shop utopia of Piazza di Spagna, 'If Dolce & Gabbana made the same suits as Armani, what would be the point? They would lose all significance.' He adds, 'An ugly girl with make-up is still ugly. And so a crappy wine put in a barrel is just wood juice.' Sobering words, indeed.

Once we've learnt our DOCs (*Denominazione di Origine Controllata*) from our DOCGs (DOC plus *Garantita*) – Italy has the strictest appellation laws in the world – Sturniolo treats the class to a bottle of Colle Gaio Frascati Superiore made way back in 1990. He rhapsodises about the care needed for a Frascati (usually drunk within two years) to have aged successfully to such complexity: 'It takes commitment to make a wine as elegant as this from a troublemaker like the Malvasia vine. At its best its rich mineral nose comes close to the king of whites, Riesling.'

The wine-tasting course, you could say in wine-label-speak, is refreshing, crisp and leaves a satisfying aftertaste. At the end of the degustation phase students climb the winding staircase – sensibly clinging to the rail if they've not used the spittoon – for a sumptuous meal in the dining room, with foods matched to the wines already tasted.

Here we are privy to such secrets as how lobster goes well with a wood-scented Chardonnay, how fish is best enhanced by a white that is not too fruity with elevated acidity, and how fettuccine with breast of quail should be served with a Grignolino or a Dolcetto.

A sense of harmony settles over the table. Someone confesses to preferring a cup of tea with her supper, and everyone laughs. The terrace opens on to the chattering technicolour of the Spanish Steps. The only thing that's missing is David Thewlis playing the piano.

1   INTERNATIONAL WINE ACADEMY OF ROMA, 8 Vicolo del Bottino, 06 699 0878, www.wineacademyroma.com. Wine-tasting courses run throughout the year.

MUSSOLINI
VINO

The grapes of wrath

Unless you are headed for the beach or Ostia Antica, you are unlikely to go anywhere near Acilia, 16km (10 miles) southwest of Rome. It's a small purpose-built suburb that forms part of Rome's ever-expanding urban rash. The road to which it clings, the Via del Mare, is known as the road of death for its frighteningly high accident and mortality rates.

Apart from the housing blocks that shimmer in the sun, there are a handful of bars, a pizza takeaway, a small supermarket and a dusty five-a-side football field, but no obvious community focus such as a sports centre or a public library. Though, bizarrely, the town attracts a travelling circus which once a year decamps its groggy tigers on wasteland not far from the graffiti-ridden station.

And yet on the trees and buildings, posters blistered by the sun show the flame of the neo-Fascist party, the Alleanza Nazionale (National Alliance), formerly the Movimento Sociale Italiano (MSI; Italian Social Movement) until it changed its name in 1994. Like so many outlying areas of Rome, Acilia's air of discrete comfort is the sort that right-wing politicians thrive on.

While Acilia is by no means as 'black' (the local euphemism for right-wing) as other zones in the city, a taste of Fascism is distilled in Bar Domino, a multi-purpose place beneath a slab of flats. According to the sign outside it's a *gelateria*, *tabacchi*, *pasticceria*, *gastronomia* and tea room all rolled into one. Despite its potential identity crisis it sounds innocent enough. And like many similar places it also sells a small stock of wine – ordinary bottles of Merlot and Pinot Nero, but with extraordinary labels: instead of the usual undulating vineyards and Bacchic images, they show the mugshots of a range of tyrants including Mussolini and Hitler (who appears on the 'Führerwein'). In case you really feel like celebrating, a bottle featuring Uncle Joe Stalin is available, too. Outnumbered by dictators, the 'Che Guevara Cabernet' seems little more than a token concession by the producers.

This historic line in wines is the brainchild of winemaker Alessandro Lunardelli. His website (www.vinilunardelli.it) offers a selection of about twenty labels of the sort that you might expect to see in a propaganda exhibition at a history museum, rather than adorning a bottle of wine.

In the puff of his own homespun PR, Lunardelli claims that he has chosen 'celebrated' figures of twentieth-century history to boost the profile of his otherwise unremarkable wine business in the northeastern city of Udine. He distributes his icon-labelled wines to just a few bars in Rome, but has begun exporting as far afield as Japan.

Understandably, Jewish organisations among others have expressed concern at the commercial use of despots' images. While a bottle of Lunardelli's vino might provide a stirring talking point at a dinner party, most people would choke at the idea of toasting men responsible for the misery and deaths of millions.

Bar Domino's owner, Rafaelle Scarano, seems at ease with this mix of wine and distasteful politics. Unashamedly Fascist, he sports a lock-jawed profile of Mussolini on his watchface and an 'Il Duce' key chain. Scarano tells me that the wine tastes good (when I try some, it is nothing special), sells consistently well and no label is more popular than any other. 'If he thinks drinking that wine will endow him with the superpower of his hero then he's drunk on the past,' says a local drily.

No one else in the bar appears outraged. There is a growing market for Mussolini merchandise among tourists and Italians alike, and Mussolini calendars and aprons, for instance, are freely sold along Rome's Via del Corso. But the two bottles bearing Hitler's image and his mindless Nationalist slogans are surely testing the limits of freedom of expression. If wine, a sacred commodity in Italy, is tainted by political incorrectness gone mad, then what's next? A Pol Pot teapot? Swastika-shaped pasta?

I wanted to buy a bottle and show it to tourists back in the centre of Rome to get some objective feedback, but I couldn't bring myself to do it. Besides at €8.30 a bottle, I could buy an inoffensive DOC wine at Trimani, guilt free.

" In the small town of Tremestieri Etneo in eastern Sicily the council proposed in 2001 to call a street 'Via Benito Mussolini – Statesman'. Throughout Italy nearly every town and city has main streets named after the country's undisputed national heroes such as Giuseppe Garibaldi and Count Camillo Cavour. But even in the current revisionist climate a Mussolini Street would have been the first of its kind in Italy. In response to public protest and outrage from as far

afield as Jerusalem and California, the proposal to
rename the street was eventually blocked.

There would be an uproar at a similar suggestion in
Rome. For years the city has borne the legacy of
Mussolini's no-nonsense roadworks – in particular Via
Fori Imperiali driven through the heart of the Roman
forums and Via del Conciliazione that razed the
medieval quarter abutting the approach to St Peter's.
Much more welcome than setting Il Duce's name in
stone are plans tabled for 'Piazza Federico Fellini',
'Via Marcello Mastroianni', and 'Via Massimo Troisi',
after the actor of *Il Postino* fame. If Italy continues to
produce such megastars of film, then maybe future
roads in honour of fallen dictators will remain the
fantasy of those drunk on the past.

ROME ON FOOT

TOSCA

Behind the scenes, and a musical walk

Opera and Italy are inseparable. The convergence of drama and music in opera creates the perfect vehicle for the swagger, sensuality and lyricism of Italy and its inhabitants. The image of an ebullient Pavarotti belting out 'Nessun Dorma', while wiping beads of sweat from his brow with a white hanky, is as Italian as Campari and soda.

Rome's history, with its Caesars, Renaissance popes and heroes of the Risorgimento, offers rich pickings for dramatists, and the composer Giacomo Puccini (1858-1924) set *Tosca*, probably the best known of 'Roman' operas, over a day and night in an unstable Rome of June 1800. The heroine, Floria Tosca, is a beautiful opera singer trapped between her lover, a painter named Mario Cavaradossi, and the menacing Chief of Police, Baron Scarpia, who discovers that Cavaradossi has helped an escaping political prisoner, Cesare Angelotti.

At the dawn of the nineteenth century the Eternal City was without a pope and was occupied by three powers: Napoleon's revolutionary forces, the old kingdom of Naples and the Vatican. Rome was no longer the powerhouse it had once been, parts of the city had fallen into neglect and its population – one million at the height of the Roman empire – had dwindled to about 150,000. In spite of its decline,

Rome remained an important religious centre with 400 churches, 250 monasteries and numerous other holy orders. On a secular note, its classical ruins, overgrown with tangled plant life, were proving popular with an emerging class of visitors from abroad.

The opera, adapted from a successful 1887 French play by Victorien Sardou, premiered in Rome at the Teatro Costanzi on 14 January 1900, a hundred years after its fictional setting. Reviews were famously unfavourable. One critic called it a 'shabby little shocker' and Benjamin Britten considered it naff and vacuous. Despite its location and intense love interest, *Tosca* is no nineteenth-century *Roman Holiday*. It has been viewed by audiences over the years as a popular soap opera dressed up as high culture – but with an 18-rated certificate. Not for the squeamish, the action depicts torture, attempted rape, murder and suicides – with none of the fairy-tale closure typical of the 1950s films that used sunny Rome as a romantic backdrop.

In fact, Rome in 1900 was the fledgling capital of a troubled nation and audiences were easily able to relate to the political instability presented onstage in *Tosca*. The king had dissolved parliament in 1899 and government forces had recently stamped out riots brought on by deteriorating economic conditions. On the eve of the premiere of *Tosca* rumours of a political assassination – Queen Margherita was among the VIPs attending – were rife.

A police officer warned the conductor that the theatre might be targeted by terrorists and, amazingly, instructed him in the event of an attack to play the national anthem. Understandably, the conductor was on tenterhooks. In fact, he ran for his life shortly after the opera began when a kerfuffle broke out in the audience. As it happened it was just a noisy argument over latecomers trying to reach their seats, and the conductor warily resumed the performance. Bravo!

Invariably the enjoyment of the opera novice is bolstered by knowing the storyline. However seductive and mellifluous Italian may sound when projected through the voicebox of a diva, it's good to know she is not just singing about ice cream. The following, then, is an outline of the opera, but as they say, if you don't wish to know the outcome, look away now.

Act One – The church of Sant'Andrea della Valle

Angelotti, having escaped from Castel Sant'Angelo where Scarpia had imprisoned him, seeks refuge in the church. Cavaradossi is at work there on a portrait of Mary Magdalene, for which his model has been the Marchesa Attavanti. He helps to hide Angelotti. Tosca arrives and is jealous of the Marchesa, but Cavaradossi manages to assure her of his love. After some stormy comings and goings, Scarpia discovers that Cavaradossi has assisted Angelotti, and as the police chief leaves he mulls over his scheme to do away with Cavaradossi and seduce Tosca.

Act Two – The police headquarters in Palazzo Farnese

Cavaradossi is arrested and brought to Scarpia, who orders his torture. Tosca arrives and on hearing her lover's screams, discloses Angelotti's hiding place and Scarpia ends his torture. But when news arrives of a battle won by Napoleon, Cavaradossi's reaction reveals his political defiance, and he is sentenced to be executed by firing squad at dawn. Tosca pleads for his life. Scarpia offers her a deal: if she sleeps with him he will spare Cavaradossi. She reaches an agreement with the police chief who, to save face, suggests faking Cavaradossi's execution. News arrives of Angelotti's suicide. As Scarpia writes letters for the couple's safe conduct, Tosca fatally stabs him with a dinner knife.

Act Three – Castel Sant'Angelo

Tosca arrives at the castle and tells everything to Cavaradossi, and the couple plan their escape. But Tosca realises she has been betrayed when her lover is shot dead by the firing squad. The soldiers have by now found Scarpia's body and they chase Tosca towards the ramparts. In despair, but still in fine voice, Tosca leaps to her death from the castle battlements.

A MUSICAL WALK

For a sight-and-sound *Tosca* walk, get hold of a personal stereo and a copy of Puccini's Roman opera on cassette or CD. The 1953 performance at La Scala in Milan, with Maria Callas, Giuseppe di Stefano, Tito Gobbi and Franco Calabrese, is the undisputed finest recording, available on EMI Classics. If you can't find this masterpiece then a €5 version from the music stall at the Campo de' Fiori market will do nicely. Then visit the three sites below for each corresponding act. (Remember to keep your music on low volume while you are in the church so as not to disturb others.)

Although 'Rome' is often given a radical makeover by contemporary directors of *Tosca*, the opera's principal settings, Sant'Andrea della Valle (Act One), Palazzo Farnese (Act Two) and Castel Sant'Angelo (Act Three), remain little altered.

Sardou set his first act in the church of Sant'Andrea al Quirinale, but Puccini chose Sant'Andrea della Valle[1] because of its proximity to the sites of the other two acts. Built in 1591 it is one of Rome's great churches, the seat of a cardinal-prince and topped by a voluminous dome which is often mistaken by tourists as that of St Peter's, the only larger cupola in the city. In Tosca's time the surrounding area would have been a warren of shady alleyways adding intrigue to the clandestine antics of Angelotti. Today, the church offers welcome peace and quiet from the thunderous traffic of Corso Vittorio Emanuele II, built just as Rome was beginning to flex its muscles as the capital of a newly united Italy.

This vast church, with a great white marble hall, glittering with gold, sumptuously decorated and lit by dust-speckled beams of light, provides a setting worthy of the emotional charge in *Tosca's* first act. While none of its four chapels, including one decorated by Michelangelo, is named after the Attavanti family as in the opera, there is a secret 'hiding place' in the Barberini chapel, the first on the left from the main entrance. The Barberini chapel also hosts the only image of Mary Magdalene in the church – not a painting, but a sixteenth-century statue by Cristoforo Stati.

Concealed in the street wall there is also a small, shallow chamber separated from the chapel proper by an ironwork grill. This is a shrine to Saint Sebastian, marking the spot where a Christian woman, Lucina, found the entrance to the city's sewers that led her to the body of the martyred saint, a brave and charitable Roman soldier who was later buried outside of the city walls in his namesake's catacombs.

Take a seat to listen to the brilliant climax of Act One in which, as a choir sings the 'Te Deum' behind him, the scheming of the villain Scarpia is absolutely woven into the music of church ritual.

Which way Angelotti would have escaped from the church is anyone's guess. If he had taken the first side street to the right on leaving the church he would have ended up in Piazza Vidoni where one of Rome's 'talking' statues, of Abbot Luigi, is set against the wall of the church. Angelotti might have used this now handless statue, originally of the Roman orator holding a scroll, to air his radical opinions (see the chapter 'Marble Oracles', page 70). Take a left, however, out of the church into Via Chiavari and veer right into Largo Pallaro. From here you can look back and survey the alarming structural cracks in the walls supporting the dome of the church.

In even worse condition is the nearby mini Baroque church to the left of a dark alleyway that leads to Piazza Biscione. Plant tendrils and weeds sprout from the church's fractured façade disguising the fact that today it is a workshop creating and selling original decorative murals for the home, grandly named the Accademia del Superfluo.[2]

The bow-shaped Via di Grotta Pina, extending to the right beyond Largo Pallaro, sits above Pompey's Theatre where Julius Caesar is thought to have been killed. Or, as the latest conspiracy theories would have us believe, where the great emperor committed suicide. Pliny the Elder tells us that Nero had the entire theatre, also the home of the Roman Curia, gilded in a single day to impress the visiting King Tiridates of Armenia. Today the forlorn piazza hosts a garage where mechanics tinker with the engines of Cinquecentos and the restaurant Da Pancrazio[3] where you can descend to the cellar and dine among the ghosts and ruins of the Imperial past. The restaurant serves classic Roman dishes.

Take either the left or right door through the dusky, covered alley. It looks spooky but is under the watchful eye of shrines to the Virgin Mary and Padre Pio, as well as a makeshift CCTV camera, that almost certainly doesn't work, as you exit on the left. On its perspiring roof faded panels of frescoes are barely discernible from when it must have been decorated like a grotto. Nowadays few local residents can recall the public scribe who once sat beneath a shabby awning in the 1930s and composed love letters for the illiterate, storing the tools of his trade in the then gated alleyway.

Turn left out of Piazza Biscione into Campo de' Fiori. Here you can assemble a *Tosca* picnic based on what fans have speculated was inside Cavaradossi's lunch basket. His packed lunch is said to have contained a loaf of bread – probably white, as the painter was a nobleman and only peasants ate brown bread – a local sheep's cheese (like the Cacio di Roma or Sini Fulvi Pastore), a farm-cured salami and a jug of wine, golden and cool like Frascati.

Just for the record, Scarpia's lavish last supper (in Act Two) would have commenced with a tray of small appetisers, such as prosciutto wrapped in colourful marzipan, savoury tartlets of nuts and greens, and small fritters of sweetbreads or, perhaps, oysters. He might have had a capon broth with tiny ravioli stuffed with capon breast, cheese, cinnamon, nutmeg, marrow and herbs, followed by a roasted whole fish filled with truffles, or hare in a sweet and sour sauce. This would have been greedily succeeded by a spit-roasted lamb. Dessert would have consisted of a sort of layered ice-cream cake with tiny biscuits and marzipan petits fours, all washed down with a sweet, mahogany coloured Oloroso sherry from Spain.

Take the street to the right of the popular wine bar La Vineria[4] into Piazza Farnese, where the most handsome

Renaissance palazzo in Rome has been home, on and off, to the French Embassy since 1635. The imposing sixteenth-century Palazzo Farnese[5] was designed by Antonio da Sangallo and its upper storeys completed by Michelangelo. The French gained exclusive rights to the palace when Italy was unified in 1871; the building was swapped for the comparatively ordinary Hotel Galiffet in Paris, for a rent of one lira payable every 99 years – surely the ultimate property bargain. Puccini transformed the upper suites of the palace into Scarpia's headquarters, where the police chief makes his indecent proposal and is stabbed by Tosca.

Occasionally during evenings when the French ambassador is hosting a dinner you can see the magnificent Carracci ceilings of the *piano nobile* (first floor) illuminated by chandeliers. If you apply to the embassy in advance, you can join a weekly visit conducted on Tuesday afternoons, usually in French.

Take a seat by one of the two basins of Egyptian granite, brought from the Baths of Caracalla and used by the Farnese family as a 'royal box' for spectacles in the square, and listen to Cavaradossi's defiant 'Vittoria!' and Tosca's heartfelt 'Vissi d'Arte'.

On the far right of the palazzo's façade is a trompe l'oeil window, from where we take the elegant Via di Monserrato, as one imagines the desperate Tosca did, en route to the castle. Puccini's heroine would have had ample opportunity to seek atonement along the way with a church every 40 metres or so on Via di Monserrato. She wouldn't, however, have had the time to rummage around the rustic art and furniture workshops or been able to hop on the no. 116 electric bus that trundles down to Via Giulia.

At no. 42 Via di Monserrato, a plaque balefully records the tragic death of a real Roman heroine, Beatrice Cenci, who was wrongly condemned of patricide and decapitated in 1599. Further on at no. 145, where Monserrato meets Via del Pelligrino, which was the medieval pilgrims' route from the city-centre hostels to the Vatican City, a carved boundary stone from the reign of Claudius adorns the wall.

Continue along Via di Monserrato as it becomes Via dei Banchi Vecchi, perhaps pausing for fortification at the *enoteca* Il Goccetto[6] before the opera's passionate denouement at Castel Sant'Angelo. Towards the end of this street the statues of angels lining the bridge, Ponte Sant'Angelo, that leads north to the castle come into view. Cross Corso Vittorio Emanuele II, walk down to the bridge and cross over it to the castle.

The castle is dominated by Emperor Hadrian's mausoleum, these days minus its marble facing and statues. Inside are three floors of richly decorated papal apartments. The Borgia rooms, the Renaissance home to the beautiful Lucrezia, her dastardly brother and their father Pope Alexander VI, have two square holes in the floor, one reputed to lead to a dungeon, the other to the River Tiber for the disposal of bodies. From the third floor a circular ramp built by Pope Gregory the Great takes you up to the terrace at the top of the castle where Puccini set his final scene.

A small, higher terrace bears a huge bronze angel in the act of sheathing his sword. The angel is a common feature in *Tosca* theatre sets. During the French occupation the statue was painted red, white and blue and a liberty cap was placed on its head. From the same platform the Campana della Misericordia (Bell of Mercy) used to announce the execution of capital sentences. When the bell tolls for Cavaradossi, Puccini takes dramatic licence by having him shot by firing squad; the usual method of execution was hanging. Likewise, at this vertiginous point of no return, with the sound of the guards' heavy footsteps behind her, Tosca is supposed to jump from here into the river, but that is clearly an impossible Olympic feat.

Listen to the lovers' final laments and enjoy the superb view stretching back to Palazzo Farnese and the dominant cupola of Sant'Andrea della Valle.

1   SANT'ANDREA DELLA VALLE, 6 Corso Vittorio, 06 686 1339, open 8am–noon & 4.30pm–7.30pm daily.
2   ACCADEMIA DEL SUPERFLUO, 21 Via di Grottapinta, 06 689 6277, www.accademiadelsuperfluo.it.
3   DA PANCRAZIO, 20 Via Grotta Pinta, 06 686 1246, www.dapancrazio.com.
4   LA VINERIA, 15 Campo de' Fiori, 06 6880 3268, open 9am–1am Mon to Sat, 5pm–1am Sun.
5   PALAZZO FARNESE, Piazza Farnese, 06 6889 2818, closed to the public, but apply in advance to join the weekly tour in French.
6   IL GOCCETTO, 14 Via dei Banchi Vecchi, 06 686 4268, open 11.30am–2pm & 5.30pm–11pm Mon to Sat.

“ At one *Tosca* production the stage hands decided to get even with the prima donna after having been subjected to her querulous tantrums during rehearsals. In the final scene, where the heroine commits suicide by leaping from the battlements of the castle, the actress's fall was usually broken by a pile of unseen mattresses. Unknown to her, the stage hands substituted a trampoline and, in this instance, to the astonishment of the audience Tosca bounced back to life.

On another occasion, at a performance in Argentina, the director was horrified to discover

during the interval that he had no guards to chase
Tosca to the battlements. Worried, he rushed out to a
nearby bar and recruited five blokes who were
hurriedly dressed backstage. As Tosca was about to
meet her end the director sent on the guards, who
proceeded to fly off the stage one by one after Tosca.

There's an added frisson to seeing *Tosca* in Rome –
even if you are not treated to such spectacular
improvisations to the plot. In summer try outdoors at
the Villa Borghese or in the magnificent setting of
Shelley's favourite hangout at the Baths of Caracalla;
otherwise don a dinner jacket or fake fur and head for
Rome's anachronistic and charming opera house, the
Teatro dell'Opera di Roma (1 Piazza B Gigli, 06 481
601, www.opera.roma.it).

CARAVAGGIO IN THE CAMPO MARZIO

The bad boy of the Baroque

Rome's churches are an eternal source of joy and surprise, from the ghoulish interior décor fashioned from monks' bones at Santa Maria della Concezione to the underground altar of an ancient Mithraic cult at San Clemente; from the geometric beauty of the Byzantine tessellated floors at San Giovanni in Laterano to the vivid frescoes depicting what seems like every conceivable torture known to man on the walls of the circular Santo Stefano Rotondo. A single lifetime is not enough to explore the hundreds of temples to saints in Rome.

Not surprisingly in a city that nurtured so many seminal artists there is a surfeit of art in its churches. This short walk around Caravaggio's old stomping ground, the Campo Marzio, highlights six of the artist's masterpieces in three churches. Not even the greatest art galleries in the world are blessed with half a dozen works by Caravaggio. In England six Caravaggios would form the basis for a major exhibition.

If one Michelangelo, the all-rounder Buonarotti of splendid Sistine Chapel and *David* sculpture fame, set the benchmark for Renaissance artists, then it was another who carried the torch into the seventeenth century for Baroque Rome. Michelangelo Merisi, however, became better known as Caravaggio, after the name of his hometown near Milan.

His revolutionary technique of tenebrism, or dramatic, selective illumination of form out of deep shadow, became a hallmark of Baroque painting. If the Baroque was a blank canvas, one day to be brimming with the work of Carracci, Domenichino, Van Dyck, Reni and Rubens, then it was Caravaggio who painted its all important first brushstrokes. Although his subjects were largely religious, he depicted his models, brought in off the streets, with a gripping realism. In the hands of Caravaggio the common people of Rome became saints and apostles.

When the young Caravaggio arrived in Rome in the late 1580s the central Campo Marzio area was a decadent neighbourhood teeming with taverns, hostels and small artists' studios. It was a city of urchins, prostitutes, card sharps and cutpurses, and street life was colourful and unpredictable. Caravaggio's early work is best remembered for fresh and direct portraits of barely draped young boys bearing baskets of fruit. These bold, seductive pictures seem to be in contrast with his own disorderly and uncertain life, living hand-to-mouth, and have subsequently fuelled academic speculation about his sexuality. After seeing Caravaggio's *Victorious Cupid*, a seventeenth-century English visitor to Rome, Richard Symonds, wrote: ''Twas the body and face of his owne boy or servant that laid with him.'

A career breakthrough came in 1595 when a dealer brought Caravaggio's work to the attention of Cardinal Francesco del Monte, a prelate of great influence in the papal court, who offered the artist board, lodging and a pension. It was probably through del Monte that Caravaggio obtained a commission in 1597 to paint his *Cycle of the Life of St Matthew* (1598-1601) in the Contarelli chapel in San Luigi dei Francesi,[1] the French national church, which lies northwest of Piazza Navona.

The church's swirling façade is almost as soot black with pollution as it is dark inside. Tourists tiptoe and fumble their way through the half light, past frescoes by Domenichino and an altarpiece by Guido Reni, to the fifth chapel on the left. Against a background of museum-like information posts, piped Bach and coin-operated illumination are three Caravaggio paintings hanging side by side where they were commissioned to be hung.

Such is the intensity of light and darkness in Caravaggio's painting that I often find myself looking over my shoulder to check that an artificial light is not being shone on the scene. This highlighting chiaroscuro effect is used in 'The Calling of St Matthew' to capture a moment when two different worlds collide.

Christ, in a shower of light and branded divine by a halo, enters a tavern with St Peter where tax collectors, dressed like peacocks and drooling over coins, are gathered around a table. A glance between Jesus and St Matthew, concentrated by the passage of light, is enough to dissolve St Matthew's old world. He draws back as if to say, 'Who, me?' while his right hand remains on the coin he had been counting, creating a tension between the venal and the holy elements of the picture.

In 'The Martyrdom of St Matthew' the eponymous event is captured just at the moment when the executioner is forcing the victim to the ground. Yet again, a dark world is suddenly and mysteriously lit up by an intense action, while at the same time it is the scene of a lowly brawl ignored by some passersby. Gone are the robes and beards of classically inspired church painting. Caravaggio is telling religious stories in a new direct way, demanding a moral choice from the ordinary people of Rome.

Like the filmmaker Pier Paolo Pasolini, who also depicted Roman low-life, Caravaggio had an eye for a cinematic moment, and unlike many of his peers he wasn't scared to swing the spotlight on to the macabre and deadly, to isolate figures and heighten the emotional tension with the threat of violence.

The first version of 'St Matthew and the Angel', the canvas that was to go over the altar, was so offensive to the canons of the church that it had to be redone. Apparently the figures lacked decorum. Even in the finished article the evangelist has the physical features of a working man equipped with large feet and a vulgar posture, while the angel is pushy rather than graceful.

On the back of the St Matthew series Caravaggio, still in his twenties, became an overnight sensation. His use of dramatic realism astonished viewers and was to become his trademark. Henceforth, and sometimes dangerously at odds with his patrons, he painted traditional religious subjects, but with a new and radical iconography and interpretation.

Leave the church and turn left into Via della Scrofa, leading to Piazza Sant'Agostino, and climb the steep steps into the church of Sant'Agostino[2] that dominates this quiet piazza. In the first chapel on your left as you enter is Caravaggio's *Madonna di Loreto*, more commonly known as *Madonna dei Pelligrini* ('Madonna of the Pilgrims', 1603–06).

Painted at the height of his powers, this graceful work of art caused a scandal because of the 'dirty feet and torn, filthy cap' of the two elderly pilgrims kneeling in the foreground. The blackened soles of the man's feet are so close to the viewer that they cannot be avoided.

From the church, guide your own well-cushioned feet along Via dei Pianellari, the lane skirting the left side of Sant'Agostino. At no. 17 you can watch sculptors shape silk-white classical busts. Next door but one at no. 19, Hostaria Pietro[3] claims to serve the best truffles in Rome – *tartufo bianco* in winter and the black variety in spring. Continue along the street veering to the right to rejoin Via della Scrofa with the Portuguese national church and a medieval tower behind you. The tower is known locally as the Torre della Scimmia, Tower of the Monkey, because back in Caravaggio's time a newly wed couple's pet monkey carried their baby to the top of the tower. After a nerve-racking stand-off the father invoked the aid of the Madonna and the monkey eventually capitulated and carefully carried the baby back down to safety. As an offering of gratitude to the Madonna, the father erected a holy shrine on the summit, which is still visible today.

On your right is Rome's favourite *tavola calda*, Volpetti.[4] It has a delicious array of hot food on display which can be eaten at the counter – try the *suppli*, deep-fried mozzarella, tomato and rice balls – and the best selection of cheese in Italy.

You should now be on course for the obelisk in the distance. To your left at no. 104a is another foodie temple, the famous Alfredo alla Scrofa[5] restaurant where the A-list has twisted its fettuccine laced with Alfredo's special cream sauce for half a century. At the junction with Piazza Nicosia a street to your right funnels down to Piazza di Spagna where its steps fan out like wings. On your left the New York architect Richard Meier has redesigned a museum space to house the Ara Pacis, a monumental Altar of Peace built by Augustus in 13 BC. A group of local architecture students have attacked it as evidence of the 'Los Angelisation of Rome'. Follow Via di Ripetta with its curious mix of shops all the way to the sweeping Piazza del Popolo.

On the Flaminio side of the piazza, to the left as you approach it, Santa Maria del Popolo[6] houses works by Raphael, Sansovino and Bernini. But it is Caravaggio's *Crucifixion of St Peter* (1600–01) and *Conversion of St Paul* (1600–01), featuring Rome's patron saints, that draw the crowds. These two sublime works face each other across the Cerasi chapel. To modern gallery-goers the pictures appear awkward, being bordered by the gaudy décor of the chapel and poorly lit by background strip lighting and a bedside lamp. Location aside, both paintings are remarkable for their photographic composition and the vivid physical presence of the characters. Although it's a shame that views are limited to a diagonal perspective.

The two paintings signal Caravaggio's artistic maturity: on the one hand, the *Conversion of St Paul* offers a forceful religious experience, while the *Crucifixion of St Peter* exemplifies the naturalism that has stunned Caravaggio's audience for centuries. Among the rippling muscles of peasants and a horse's rump are the trademark dirty feet of a stooped executioner – a reminder that Piazza del Popolo was the site of public executions until the late nineteenth century.

More of Caravaggio's works can be seen in Rome, for a small fee, at the Pinacoteca Capitolina (Capitoline Art Gallery),[7] the Galleria Borghese[8] and the Galleria Doria Pamphilj (see page 119).

Caravaggio was essentially an anarchic soul at odds with the world of cardinals and princes that clothed and fed him. It seemed that as his reputation as a painter grew, so did his propensity for brushes with the law. The 'Bad Boy of the Baroque' carved a second career out of disputes and GBH. Two records from 1604 show that he was accused of flinging a plate of artichokes in the face of a waiter and arrested for throwing stones at Roman guards. His violent temper makes today's headline grabbing artists appear saintly by comparison.

In 1606 he finally killed a man in a rage after a game of tennis. He inflicted the fatal wound as he attempted to cut off his opponent's testicles with a sword – allegedly the man was the pimp of a prostitute who had won Caravaggio's affections. Research has shown that the artist was avenging his honour in a way that was totally in keeping with the culture of the Rome of his day. Four hundred years ago if a man insulted another man's reputation he might have his face slashed; if he abused another man's woman he might expect to lose his manhood. A recent headline in the *Daily Telegraph*, from an article explaining the above, claimed: 'Red-blooded Caravaggio killed love rival in bungled castration attempt'.

For the rest of his life Caravaggio was on the run. Naples, Malta (where he was imprisoned for beating a knight to within a sliver of death) and Sicily all provided refuge for short periods. Dishevelled and longing for Rome, he nevertheless continued to produce outstanding works, many of which reflected his flighty existence with a subdued tone and a delicacy of emotion.

In 1609, however, he was attacked at an inn and wounded so badly that news reached Rome that the 'celebrated painter' was dead. Clinging to life and determined to return to Rome, by the following year he had reached the mouth of the Tiber. But fate was to deny him rest in the Eternal City. Feverish and exhausted he died in pursuit of his few worldly goods that had somehow left without him for the port of Naples.

1 SAN LUIGI DEI FRANCESI, 5 Piazza San Luigi dei Francesi, 06 688 271, open 8.30am–12.30pm & 3.30pm–7pm daily, but closed Thurs afternoons.

2 SANT'AGOSTINO, Piazza Sant'Agostino, 06 6880 1962, open 8am–noon & 4pm–7.30pm daily.

3 HOSTARIA PIETRO, 19 Via dei Pianellari, closed Sun.

4 VOLPETTI, 31 Via della Scrofa, 06 686 1940, open 8am–8.15pm daily, except Sun.

5 ALFREDO ALLA SCROFA, 30 Piazza Augusto Imperatore, 06 687 8734, closed Sun.

6 SANTA MARIA DEL POPOLO, 12 Piazza del Popolo, 06 361 0836, open 7am–noon & 4pm–7pm Mon to Sat, 8am–1.30pm & 4.30pm–7.30pm Sun.

7 PINACOTECA CAPITOLINA, 1 Piazza del Campidoglio, 06 6710 2071, open 9.30am–8pm daily, except Mon.

8 GALLERIA BORGHESE, 5 Piazzale Scipione Borghese, 06 32 810, open 8.30am–7pm daily, except Mon.

MARBLE ORACLES

Conversations with 'talking' statues

Italians love to talk, and Rome's fraternity of 'talking' statues is proof of its people's irrepressible need to voice a point of view. Since the days when taking a pop at the pope in public was a risky business, punishable at the stake or gallows, the statues have been used by citizens as a sort of Post-It board to vent their feelings about those in power.

The tradition began in 1501 shortly after the death of Pasquino, a local tailor renowned for his sharp wit. A third-century BC torso of Menelaus shielding the slain body of Patroclus was unearthed and erected near his shop, just off Piazza Navona, towards Corso Vittorio Emanuele II.

Initially the statue performed an official function: being on a route used by pilgrims, it was often allegorically masked and garlanded with Latin poems to edify the people. The locals soon caught on and, overnight, placards carrying irreverent and sarcastic messages, often in Roman dialect, began to appear on the statue. In memory of the radical tailor the battered torso became known affectionately as Pasquino – from which we derive the English word 'pasquinade' – and its small square became Piazza di Pasquino.

The days before a free press and a united Italy were a golden age for Pasquino, when unpopular popes were often the targets of barbed comments affixed to the statue. Pope Urbanus VIII Barberini found himself in the line of fire when he raided Ancient Roman monuments to beautify St Peter's basilica, and to add insult to injury, also raised taxes for the working classes. When he ordered the Pantheon's portico to be stripped of its gilt bronze ceiling trusses in order to make cannon and allow Bernini to fashion a lavish *baldacchino* (canopy) above the altar of St Peter's, the following message appeared on Pasquino: 'Quod non fecerunt Barbari, fecerunt Barberini' ('What the Barbarians didn't do, Barberini did').

When Sixtus V became pope in 1585, Pasquino was dressed in a soiled shirt. An excuse written beneath it explained that he was forced to wear foul linen because his laundress had become a princess. This was a reference to the Pope's sister who, before the elevation of her brother, had been a washerwoman. The act caused an uproar in Rome and the Pope offered a handsome reward to anyone who revealed the guilty satirist. The author, believing the Pope to be a respecter of honesty, handed himself in. The Pope remained good to his word and handed over the bounty of one thousand doubloons. But in order to ensure that the incident would not be repeated, he had the satirist's tongue removed and both his hands chopped off.

Despite such incidents, other platforms for spouting off flourished. The practice expanded to a huge statue of a river god known as Marforio which had been hauled into Piazza Campidoglio from the Forum of Mars. Today Marforio sits in stony silence in a courtyard of the nearby Capitoline Museum. From Piazza di Pasquino, walk east along Corso Vittorio Emanuele II, turning right at Piazza del Gesù into Via Coeli, and on to Piazza Campidoglio.

The dissenting scribes used Marforio when it was impossible to make Pasquino 'talk' because of the papal guards watching him. The statues, a ten-minute stroll apart, struck up a rapport. They would enter into 'conversations', with one providing an ironic reply to questions posed by the other about the hot-potato issues of the day.

Head down from the Campidoglio and turn right into Piazza San Marco. In the corner of this unprepossessing space exposed to traffic, just around the block from the balcony of Palazzo Venezia from which Mussolini frequently bellowed, slumps the colossal bust of Madame Lucrezia, the only female among Rome's stony group of chatterboxes. Originally a statue of Isis, it takes its present name from Lucrezia d'Alagno, a fifteenth-century courtesan who lived in the area and was probably a notorious harbinger of gossip.

From Piazza Venezia head down Via del Corso and on the first left, secreted in shady Via Lata, is another marble oracle. Il Facchino, the porter or water-carrier, has been lodged in the side wall of a Bank of Rome building since 1872. In the Middle Ages, after the Roman aqueducts had been cut by the invading barbarians, water-carriers (known as *acquaioli* or *acquaroli*) carried water from the Tiber to the city's inhabitants – until their work dried up after the popes restored the aqueducts in the sixteenth century.

The humble Il Facchino was vociferous during the Risorgimento in the nineteenth century, when the Romans were fighting to obtain freedom from the temporal power of the pope and pasquinades were used as an important means of informing and inciting the people. According to tradition the Renaissance statue has the features of Martin Luther, who stayed in Rome in 1511 – but today his face is puggish and flattened from constant tactile abuse.

These days, the most 'talkative' of all the talking statues is on Via del Babuino near the Spanish Steps — continue along Via del Corso and turn right into Via dei Greci. The pockmarked statue is said to be of the reclining Silenus, a bearded faun, half-man and half-goat and drinking pal of Bacchus, the god of wine and revelry. The statue is so ugly that when it was placed in what was Via Paulina in the sixteenth century, the locals immediately nicknamed it Il Babuino — the baboon — and the street came to be named after it. Comments usually fill the wall behind the statue like a message board and even spread round the corner into the side street. But the last time I passed by, Il Babuino had been gagged — the wall had been sprayed with a glossy anti-graffiti paint.

However, the comments are creeping back. According to the adjacent florist, much of the commentary is attributable to a local artist who works in the parallel Via Margutta. He also leaves calling-card stickers on the wall advertising his latest exhibitions. Otherwise the 'talk' is mostly political, a war of words waged between youths from the left and right, and reflections on the latest political scandals. Arguably Il Babuino lowers the tone for the neighbouring slew of antiques dealers, but it makes an unorthodox, if sometimes slightly obtuse, alternative to the newspapers bulging with opinions at the newsstand nearby.

When all's said and done, it's good to know that if the traffic and heat conspire against you and you're struggling to express yourself in Italian, relief is on hand. You can always post your grievances on one of the city's talking statues.

TRASTEVERE TRAIL

Poets and piazzas

Trastevere, literally meaning 'across the *Tevere*' or Tiber, is a picturesque 'village' nestled into a bend on the east bank of Rome's muddy river. Tranquil during the day, animated after sundown, in parts achingly beautiful, in others rundown, it is more than a match for its well-trodden neighbours in the *centro storico*. It is also – with the exception of Viale Trastevere, the byway that splices the neighbourhood in two – a relatively traffic-free zone by Rome's standards.

Once the stronghold of working-class Trasteverini, said to be the most Roman of Romans with their own coarse dialect and distinctive Festa de Noantri ('We Others' celebration) each summer, the area is now firmly in its post-Bohemian phase. In the main, foreign students and wealthy Italians inhabit its beamed apartments, but vestiges of its former life can still be glimpsed.

The walk begins in Piazza G Gioacchino Belli, just south of Ponte Garibaldi, alongside the marble statue of a man who sketched nineteenth-century Trasteverini in verse. Giuseppe Gioacchino Belli (1791–1863) has been called Rome's 'one and only great poet'. He wrote more than two thousand sonnets in Romanesque, the language of the common people:

> My purpose is to set down the verbal idiom of the
> Roman just as it issues from his mouth, without
> ornament or alteration, without correcting its syntax
> or its licence . . . In my work I portray the ideas of a
> class of people which, though ignorant, is yet
> brimming with strong opinion, is shrewd, and
> hereditarily inclined to sarcasm, to epigram, to a
> mode of speech which is proverbial and concise.[1]

The statue of Belli (1913) by Michele Tripisciano
seems dressed for a night on the town with his cane, top hat
and tailed overcoat. Sit to his left and you can see our final
destination, Garibaldi's statue on the crest of the Janiculum
hill, which from here seems suspended in mid air.

Fittingly at this ceaseless traffic hub, the plinth of
Belli's statue bears a herm of the four-headed Roman deity
Janus, who guards over entrances and all beginnings.
Concealed behind the statue is an interesting relief, a
tableau of a crowd of Romans enjoying a poem posted on
the famous talking statue Pasquino. Such poems, which
invariably poked fun at the state and its cronies, were the
sort penned by Belli himself.

Notice, about 50 metres behind Belli's statue, an
ancient Ionic column embedded into the side of the house
at no. 22 Via di San Bonosa. It is an example of how Roman
artefacts of inestimable value have been used for both
decorative and structural purposes throughout the city.

Moving along Viale Trastevere, next on the left is the
thirteenth-century Palazzetto dell' Anguillara, a rare
example of a medieval house in Rome. Known as the Casa
di Dante, it is certainly old enough to support the myth that
the celebrated Tuscan stayed here when he visited Rome,

and it is now a centre for the study of the poet. With its crenellated tower and rusted iron torch holders above the door and windows, it is like a castle marooned among the traffic. On the Via della Lungaretta side of the palazzo a tablet records the depth beneath the ground of the local underground stream, Acqua Paola.

Cross Viale Trastevere, taking care to avoid its new aeroplane-like trams, to the church opposite. San Crisogno has a kaleidoscopic marble floor, made from fragments scavenged by the Cosmati brothers, and lining the aisle are ancient Ionic columns topped with playful capitals. To the left of the nave is the sacristry where, for an offering of €2, a church warden will open a door and you can descend 10 metres all alone to the remains of an early-Christian church dating from the third century. In this dank chamber of aged artefacts you are reminded, yet again, that wherever you tread in Rome an ancient city lies beneath your step. If you go when there is a mass in the church above, the muffled sound of footsteps and the organ lends an uncanny atmosphere to the experience.

Back at street level, turn left along Via della Lungaretta and then left again into Piazza San Rufino winding your way to the haven that is Via dei Fienaroli. At no. 31d is Rome's only bookshop for women, Il Tempo Ritrovato,[2] and further down at no. 28 is Bibli,[3] a mini literary village where you can be bookish while savouring the most wholesome home-made food in Rome in its garden café.

Return to Via della Cisterna and its delightful barrel-and-carafe fountain emblazoned with the Roman SPQR, 'Senatus Populusque Romanus' ('The Senate and People of Rome'). The fountain is not a Roman antique, but even today the local council uses the Imperial motto on municipal goods from drain covers to stationery. Naturally, northern Italians find it pretentious and prefer '*Sono Porchi Questi Romani*' ('They are pigs these Romans') or '*Sa il Podesta Quanto ha Rubato*' ('Only the governor knows how much he has stolen'). Note also the darkened faux windows above and to the right of the fountain.

Continue ahead into the misshapen Piazza San Calisto, which at peak times has the appearance of a sunken car park. The blackened and defunct-looking church transforms into a sort of charity shop on Sundays, selling second-hand furs and wedding dresses.

The no-nonsense Bar San Calisto on the right (see page 24 in the 'Caffè' chapter) is now unstylishly at odds with the gentrification of the district, a process that started in the late 1950s when artists and foreigners came to live here, attracted by the ramshackle beauty and then low rents. Now artisans' workshops are outnumbered by boutiques, art galleries and fancy bars, with a new venture opening almost every week.

From the bar, veer right into Piazza Santa Maria in Trastevere, the district's centre stage and pulsating heart. On a Saturday night it feels as though the whole of Rome is gathered here linked arm in arm for the ritual *passeggiata*. The piazza brims with characters: a ragged *contadino* (peasant) who has walked in from the outlying *campagna* with a cart full of roasting sweetcorn and chestnuts; a toothless Chinese man with his magic box of lighters and contraband cigarettes; a beautiful gipsy girl with armfuls of Cellophane-wrapped roses ready to thrust at passing lovers; and fire-eaters, fortune-tellers, and a suitably gaunt, but enterprising, poet offering neat scrolls of his verse for sale.

Overseeing this excess of secular activity is the fourth-century Santa Maria in Trastevere. The church is adorned with golden mosaics of the apostles, and is a prime example of how the different layers of history are fused together in many of Rome's buildings. Adjoining the church is a vast, neglected palazzo – a Vatican outpost – covered in a film of grime and frayed posters, against which children and soldiers play football in the early evening. The palazzi opposite with their *gelato*-coloured façades and windows brimming with pretty flowers offer good examples of the twentieth-century addition of a rooftop to these older buildings. On the other side of the piazza, opposite the church, is Sabatini,[4] a ritzy restaurant with outdoor seating where rich tourists indulge themselves. A sequence filmed here in Fellini's *Roma* has the American writer Gore Vidal, stirred by the city's inescapable associations with the past and 'decline', gloomily claim this to be 'as good a place as any to wait for the end of the world'.

A more modest spot from which to ponder mortality and people-spectate, is the steps of the Roman fountain in the centre of the piazza. A favourite meeting place and a magnet for riff-raff, it's the perfect place to watch Italians unfailingly preening themselves in the large mirror of the restaurant adjacent to Sabatini's.

Cross the piazza to Via della Fonte d'Olio – the street is named after the legend behind the founding of the church of Santa Maria when a font of oil sprang here on Christ's birthday. Pass the back entrance to the Pasquino,[5] a well-concealed English-language cinema. It has a sliding roof from which cats have been known to drop on to unsuspecting members of the audience. Continue down Vicolo del Piede to Piazza de' Renzi with its tattered rows of flags left over from when Roma won the championship, and its earthy bonhomie of Da

Augusto's *trattoria* (see the 'Da Augusto' chapter, page 10). Take Via della Pelliccia to Via del Moro.

On your left are some interesting independent shops. At no. 45 the renamed Almost Corner Bookshop[6] (recently moved from its former corner location) is a genial stock-piled English bookshop no bigger than a bedroom. Further down at no. 59 is Polvere di Tempo,[7] where the owner Adrian Rodriguez, an architect and craftsman, makes charming gifts inspired by time, such as handcrafted hourglasses, sundials, globes and kaleidoscopes.

The street plaque in the piazza named after the native satirical poet Trilussa reveals his real name to be 'Carlo Alberto Salustri, 1871–1950'. Trilussa – another of 'modern' Rome's most beloved poets along with Belli – devised his pen name from an anagram of his family name. Pass the Friends bar, its entrance topped by a Latin inscription, and if you are hungry pause at the Pizza Trilussa takeaway which is quite simply poetry in dough and toppings. Slake your thirst at the street-level Acqua Paola fountain, which echoes the three arches of its larger sister fountain on the Janiculum hill, visible from the nearby Ponte Sisto. Just beyond, on a grassy segment where tramps bed down, is an engaging monument to Trilussa: a bronze statue on a marble plinth. It has the poet holding forth while leaning over a collage of Roman fragments, his huge hand curled in gesticulation. Either side of his haughty Roman nose the red and yellow stripes of Roma football club have been daubed on his cheeks.

Like Belli, Trilussa was a dialect poet, though his work is softer sounding. Popular in the 1920s and 1930s, he preferred taverns to literary circles and found his inspiration on the street, often using animal imagery to highlight man's foibles. The poem to the right of his statue about a man observing the bestial locals from beneath the shade of an umbrella is typical of his coarse style.

Take Via di Ponte Sisto and pick up Via di Santa Dorotea until you reach Caffè Settimiana. If you haven't lunched yet this is a good place to refuel before the walk up Via Garibaldi.

Before the ascent take a mini digression left at Via del Mattonato and wander around this enchanting block of backstreets lined with washing and pennants. On your first left is Vicolo della Scala. As far as I know the delightful family restaurant at no. 8 has no name; it is little more than a kitchen open to the public, where Roman housewives cook and their menfolk carry the dishes. Return to Via Garibaldi.

Take the steps where the road bends and turn right into Via di Porta San Pancrazio. Its steep gradient should help you to work off the pizza or pasta. On your left is the grand early-Baroque Acqua Paola fountain which flows down to its smaller namesake fountain below (and which recently underwent a facelift). Its stupendous outlook over the city is popular with TV advertisers. The lofty Spanish ambassador's residence immediately below is testimony to Iberian influence in Rome down through the ages.

Continue up the hill, turning right through the gates into the Passeggiata del Gianicolo. A row of stern, bearded busts of Garibaldi's men line the way to the summit where a majestic statue of their leader – the speck that we saw at the beginning of the walk – rides a horse above the slogan 'Roma o morte' ('Rome or death'). It was in Trastevere that Garibaldi found the most ardent support for his valiant defence of republican Rome against the French in 1849.

Curiously one of Garibaldi's Red Shirts was a Cornish fisherman, John Peard, who was frequently mistaken as the big man himself. His sculptured features are opposite the Finnish embassy and in good company. Behind him is a statue of Garibaldi's feisty wife, Anita. In the best tradition of the spaghetti western, she is poised on a bolting colt, somehow waving a pistol in the air while at the same time clutching a baby.

These days less fiery newly weds parade the confetti-strewn piazza. They come here for a view that poets have been praising for two thousand years and which, although due east, sets Rome alight at sunset.

1   From the Introduction to *Roman Sonnets* by Giuseppe Gioacchino Belli, translated by Harold Norse, Highlands, 1960.

2   IL TEMPO RITROVATO, 31d Via dei Fienaroli, 06 581 7724, open 3.30pm–7.30pm Mon, 10am–1pm & 3.30pm–7.30pm Tues to Sat.

3   BIBLI, 28 Via dei Fienaroli, 06 588 4097, www.bibli.it, open 5.30pm–midnight Mon, 11am–midnight Tues to Sun.

4   SABATINI, 13 Piazza Santa Maria in Trastevere, 06 581 2026, open noon–3pm & 7pm–midnight daily.

5   PASQUINO, 10 Piazza Sant'Egidio, 06 581 5208, www.multisalapasquino.com.

6   THE ALMOST CORNER BOOKSHOP, 45 Via del Moro, 06 583 6942, open 10am–1.30pm & 3.30pm–8pm daily.

7   POLVERE DI TEMPO, 59 Via del Moro, 06 588 0704, open 10am–8pm Mon to Sat.

IN THE FOOTSTEPS OF FASCISM

A tour of Mussolini's Rome

As an antidote to the all pervasive antiquity of the city here are some signposts for a flavour of Fascist Rome. As a walk it breaks down into three parts, which can be done together over the course of a day by taking both metro lines and a bus, or completed separately.

The two main settlements of Fascist Rome are at opposite ends of the city. About 6km (4 miles) south of the city centre, EUR (Esposizione Universale di Roma) was conceived in 1938 as a showcase of Fascist architecture for the 1942 World Expo. The expo was cancelled because of World War II and much of the work was finished in the 1950s evolving into a breezy blend of public buildings and well-to-do apartments.

In the northwest of Rome between Monte Mario and the Tiber is the Foro Italico, a sporting complex that now flanks the current Olympic stadium. Between the two main settlements, and forming the middle part of this tour, the stations and post office in and around Porta San Paolo constitute a pocket of buildings worth a look.

For EUR take metro B to its penultimate stop, EUR Fermi. You surface into what feels like an alternative satellite city, a sort of grand-scale Milton Keynes a million miles away in feel from the knotty confines of medieval Rome. Behind you are the 'Fungo', or 'Mushroom', a water tower topped with a panoramic restaurant, and the revamped UFO shaped Palasport, a concert and sports venue.

Wander the sweeping avenues lined with stark Rationalist buildings and neat hedges – I think getting lost here enhances the 'alien' aspect of its landscape. The pared-back classicism of such buildings blown up to a monumental scale indicated Fascism's conformist values and Imperial pretensions. As a marker, the district's network of boulevards intersects in Piazza Marconi around a modern obelisk of white Carrara marble, 40 metres high.

EUR's reputation as a second-rate museumland is a bit harsh. It does, after all, have central Rome to compete with. There are, in fact, plenty of interesting things to see here if you have the time to sift through the cavernous, often people-free, halls of museums dedicated to traditional handicrafts, ethnography, medieval art, and post and tele-communications. The assured 'Square Colosseum' (the Palazzo della Civiltà del Lavoro, to give it its proper name), a compact skyscraper of row after row of Roman arches, is worth the visit alone to EUR. Current external repairs are expected to continue until the end of 2005, after which plans are afoot to turn this equally loved and loathed building into an audiovisual museum. Hopefully it will inspire EUR Spa, the area's landlords, to mend the leaking roof and put the heating on in winter. For the time being, the building keeps a 1:250 scaled-down plastic model of Constantine's Rome in its basement, without a doubt the *capolavoro* (masterpiece) of all the zone's museums. To see what looks like plastic on a grander scale, the mighty dome of the Santi Pietro e Paolo church, a tribute to Michelangelo's first plans for St Peter's based on a Greek cross, is visible from the palazzo.

Head to the fantastic café, Palombini,[1] at the foot of the staircase to the 'Square Colosseum' for a chance to digest EUR's unique lesson in European town planning – and to contemplate the construction of the area's latest building, Massimiliano Fuksas's looming glass-fronted convention centre, complete with a cloud-like suspended main meeting hall.

Rather in keeping with Fascist treatises on the benefits of turbo-charged bravado, the quarter has lately suffered from a bout of clandestine street car racing at night. Italian newspapers also reported, in October 2003, the rediscovery of 'Mussolini's secret bunker', an air-raid shelter underneath EUR Spa's headquarters in Largo Virgilio Testa. At the mention of the 'discovery' Nunzio Carretta, a property manager at the company, shakes his head. 'We always knew it was there,' he says with a tired smile. 'Someone just happened to dig up the architectural plans for the building in the Archivio di Stato [State Archives].'

For the second part of our tour, take the metro back to Piramide station, near Porta San Paolo. To your left when you exit Piramide is the station for the electric railway to Ostia. Opened in 1921, it was part of Mussolini's plan to extend Rome to the sea and was the first station in Italy to have its platform level with the train. The ticket hall behind its simple classical façade is blessed by a Gabriele D'Annunzio poem singing the praises of the Fascist life-style. Murals of Neptune and crab motifs decorate the walls, and the ticket booths are surrounded with original polished oak. In contrast to the station's olde-worlde brand of Fascist design, across the busy piazza on the Aventine side of Via Marmorata is the slick Fascist-era post office built in 1933 by Adalberto Libera and Mario de Renzi, its diagonally etched concrete façade echoing the bound Fasces of the regime's emblem.

To your right when you exit Piramide, in Piazzale dei Partigiani, is Ostiense mainline train station. With none of the bold ostentation of, say, the Fascist-built Milan central station, this low-slung terminus for southbound trains is often spookily quiet for its size. Its interesting décor includes Modernist lamps and butch warrior mosaics on the pavement beneath the entrance canopy.

More faux-antique mosaics of this sort can be seen at the Foro Italico, an ambitious sports centre built to Imperial designs on Mussolini's orders in 1928–31. To get there you will need to take the metro to Lepanto, changing at Termini, and then a no. 32 bus to Ponte Duca d'Aosta.

Again, it is probably best to roam this area, which is much smaller than EUR, at your leisure. If you are here on a day when Roma or Lazio aren't playing at home you will most likely have the place to yourself. An obelisk, controversially still inscribed with 'Mussolini Dux', greets you on the walkway to the stadium. Il Duce would have preferred a colossal statue of himself, but plans for that project were shelved when they ran out of bronze.

All around you are concrete examples of Mussolini's body Fascism. The pot-bellied leader was obsessed with the idea that his people should look vigorous and warlike. Black and white mosaics depicting Romans hunting and wrestling, some of which have now been sledgehammered,

line the marbled approach to the modern stadium. While to
the right of the stadium, the open Stadio dei Marmi
(Stadium of Marbles) sports around its perimeter a ring of
sixty colossal statues of athletes. Real-life athletes that you
might see around here are mostly joggers, but the whole
area transforms into an outdoor sports centre and night-life
village during the summer.

Nearby, between Viale delle Olimpiade and Viale dei
Gladiatori, is the Tennis Club Foro Italico,[2] which hosts the
Italian Open tennis tournament each May. Conveniently it
has a bar inside that's open to the public. Yet more statues of
perfectly proportioned young soldiers line the route down
to the architecturally stylish, though slightly shabby, 1930s
Foro Italica Youth Hostel. From here you can catch bus no.
32 or 280, or from across the bridge tram no. 2, back to the
city centre.

1   PALOMBINI, 12 Piazzale Adenauer, 06 591 1700, open 7am–midnight
    daily.
2   TENNIS CLUB FORO ITALICO, 31 Viale dei Gladiatori, 06 3685
    8218.

THE MONTI QUARTER

An up-and-coming neighbourhood

The decadent hub of the Monti neighbourhood (or *rione* Monti), bounded by Via Cavour, Via dei Serpenti and Via Panisperna, is a compact, atmospheric place perfect for an afternoon of milling around its eclectic shops.

The area's notorious tenement blocks were built for the poor at the turn of the last century around the site of the Suburra, the crowded slums of Ancient Rome. Until 1958 – when the Merlin Law saw the abolition of their state regulation and led to their closure – they housed raucous brothels, or 'houses of tolerance', of the sort seen in the opening sequence of Fellini's *Roma*. Some old Romans still speak with frank nostalgia of their visits to these bordellos. They also attest to the quarter's nexus of *botteghe* (workshops) where artisans made stained glass, furniture, lampshades, tapestries and suits.

Many *botteghe* have disappeared, but some of their shop-signs are still evident above doorways today. Local craftsmen such as the tapestry maker Silvio Clemente Rovati are always happy to exchange a few words about their trade, though they lament their lack of keen successors among young people.

Although ramshackle and old, *rione* Monti is neither preciously embalmed in its ancient history nor has it yet been overrun with foreigners. Dead-end streets of steep steps and tenements creeping with ivy characterise this once working-class area which is discovering its own cultural beat. According to the local press, film stars have been moving into the area for its 'unspoilt charm and authenticity'.

All sorts of shops are racked up along Via del Boschetto. A greengrocer's that will take orders via the Internet and a gay bazaar, Libreria Queer, share the street with nimble-fingered cobblers and seamstresses who still make a living by repairing things. At no. 61 you can buy works from the studio of one of Italy's most influential illustrators, Chiara Rapaccini, the wife of the film director Mario Monicelli.

Not far away at no. 1 is Le Brebis Noire,[1] one of the city's first shops for hand-woven fabrics, opened in 1979 by a French woman, Florence Quellin, who uses an antique wooden loom to hand weave delicate cloth and fabrics for clothes, coats and scarves. At Archivia[2] studio and store, at no. 15, you can rummage for unusual decorative objects, interesting mirrors, lamps made out of salt-corroded copper, and plates decorated by famous artists. And if you like pretty knick-knacks, Fabio Piccioni[3] at no. 148 has stacks of Tupperware containers full of coloured stones and beads which he uses to make his own jewellery.

Turn left off Via del Boschetto into Via Panisperna. If by now you need some retail respite in the form of a drink, an attractive option is the Charity Café[4] at no. 68 which doubles up as a tea room in the afternoon and a jazz club by night. Alternatively, on nearby Via dei Serpenti, Al Vino Al Vino[5] is a popular wine bar specialising in fine grappas. At the crossroads of Via Panisperna and Via dei Serpenti, note the terrific views of the Colosseum at one end of the street and the church of Santa Maria Maggiore at the other.

Pick up Via degli Zingari where there's a plaque commemorating the Romany gipsies who died alongside the Jews in the Holocaust, '. . . that it may never happen again, that it may never be forgotten, and that brotherhood among all peoples be sustained'. Turn the corner into Via dell'Angeletto. Escat[6] is a small boutique that sells rare vintage clothing with oriental tunics from the turn of the last century, coats from the 1930s, purses in damask, sophisticated costume jewellery and shoes.

From Via dell'Angeletto you come upon Via Leonina where La Bottega del Cioccolato[7] makes notable miniatures of Roman monuments – the Colosseum in white chocolate has a rich, buttery vanilla taste. Con e Senza Zucchero[8] is a deli that sells Roman honey, balsamic vinegar, oils and organic produce – and, not to everyone's taste, sugar- and fat-free *cantucci* biscuits. Across the street is Tablo, where a skilled craftsman makes and decorates original and affordable wooden picture frames of all sorts and sizes.

A left turn leads you back into the beguiling fifteenth-century Piazza Suburra. But turning right, instead, leads into the equally alluring Piazza della Madonna dei Monti. Back on the lively Via dei Serpenti is Maharajan,[9] an Indian restaurant that merits two forks in the authoritative Michelin guide. No doubt it is a favourite haunt of the thespians who run the English Theatre of Rome[10] on Via Urbana, which has shows in English at 9pm every Friday from October to June – during the summer funny things happen at the Roman Forum when the Miracle Players perform comic theatre in English among the classical ruins.

1   LE BREBIS NOIRE, 1 Via del Boschetto, 06 482 0357.

2   ARCHIVIA, 15a Via del Boschetto, 06 474 1503, open
     9.30am–1.30pm & 4.30pm–7.30pm daily, except Mon am.

3   FABIO PICCIONI, 148 Via del Boschetto, 06 474 1697.

4   CHARITY CAFÉ, 68 Via Panisperna, 06 4782 5881.

5   AL VINO AL VINO, 19 Via dei Serpenti, 06 485 803.

6   ESCAT, 10 Via dell'Angeletto, 06 474 5721.

7   LA BOTTEGA DEL CIOCCOLATO, 82 Via Leonina, 06 482 1473.

8   CON E SENZA ZUCCHERO, 81 Via Leonina, 06 482 0533.

9   MAHARAJAN, 124 Via dei Serpenti, 06 474 7144, open for lunch
     12.30pm–3pm Mon to Sat, for dinner 7pm–midnight daily.

10   ENGLISH THEATRE OF ROME, 107 Via Urbana, 06 488 5608. For
     the Miracle Players' summer performances at the Roman Forum,
     06 7039 3427, www.miracleplayers.org.

SHOPPING SECRETS

DESIGNER SHOPS AND FLEA MARKETS

From boutiques to bargains

Rome's primary high-street shopping areas are along the three main thoroughfares Via del Corso, Via Nazionale and Via Cola di Rienzo (north of Castel Sant'Angelo), as well as the area around Piazza di Spagna, and Via Condotti which runs off to the southwest of the piazza.

Although savvy seekers of retail therapy shop during the week, the bustle in the streets around Via Condotti on a Saturday afternoon is a sight to behold. The whole area swarms with shoppers dressed to thrill; they creak with leather and leave in their wake the ricocheted tic-tac sound of stilettos. While the meticulous window displays showcasing the latest styles almost raise consumerism to an art form, teenage window-shoppers hover outside the Armani and Gucci emporiums, enviously eyeing the gleeful Japanese tourists laden with shiny designer bags. Shopping in these stores is very much a look-but-don't-touch experience, but also a great lesson in what's new in interior design.

The best way to escape the disapproval of the robotic shop assistants and avoid paying a king's ransom for a pair of shoes is to take the underground to San Giovanni where, in the shadows of the ancient Aurelian gate and wall, the market in Via Sannio is a maze of stalls offering retro clothing, discontinued originals and copied designer clothes as well as factory seconds with barely distinguishable flaws. The covered part of the market sells designer sporting goods, branded Italian shoes, handbags and other leather items, and there are bargains to be had with sunglasses, shoes and camping gear. The market opens from 10am to 1.30pm Monday to Thursday, and until 6pm on Saturday.

If you simply must have designer labels, then visit the market in Viale Parioli in north Rome's upmarket Parioli area, reached by bus no. 3 or 53. Starting with fresh fruit and vegetable stalls in Via Locchi, the market shifts into stalls offering bargain household items, leather goods, shoes and clothing, including, for example, excellent copies of Prada sportswear — the goods are produced in Naples and then sold as 'non-authentic'. Bearing in mind that many designer products are made in faraway countries where production costs are minimal, it's surely more 'authentic' to buy 'Made in Italy' copies. Though be sure to avoid hawk-eyed fashionistas who can spot a fake a catwalk away. The market opens 8am to 2pm Monday to Saturday.

Every Sunday, from 5am to 2pm, the quiet streets in Trastevere's southwest corner come to life with Rome's biggest, most chaotic flea market. Porta Portese market winds for more than 3km (2 miles) from the ancient gate near the Tiber at Piazza di Porta Portese, along the Via Portuense and the streets enclosed by Viale Trastevere. Featured in Vittorio De Sica's neorealist classic *Ladri di*

Biciclette (*The Bicycle Thieves*, 1948) – the father and son come here to search in vain for their stolen bike – the market touts everything from Gucci watch parts to busts of Mussolini, and is a great place to brush up on the Ancient Roman pastimes of bargaining and arguing.

What started as a black market after World War II has mushroomed into a crowded bargain-fest with bootleg music, mismatched silver, antique postcards, adult comic books and, along side streets, Russian immigrants offering Soviet cameras and medals. It's the first port of call for the *trovarobe* ('finder of things') when a film director requests an object – a Victorian iron, an Art Deco lamp or newspapers from a bygone age, for example – that can't be found in the storerooms of Cinecittà Studios. It is also where your car radio or mobile phone is likely to be hawked if it has been stolen – though you'd be unlikely to find it among the dense crowd.

In the past decade alone there have been some startling finds at Porta Portese. Police have recovered £2 million worth of stolen paintings and statues, much of which came from churches in southern Italy. Paintings, including three scenes of the Stations of the Cross done in the style of the school of Caravaggio, and a seventeenth-century crucifix, had been sliced into smaller pieces to avoid detection. One art critic even stumbled upon a trove of original Raphael drawings.

You needn't be looking for anything in particular to enjoy this boisterous human circus. However, it's wise to keep hold of your wallet and beware the market's assorted scam artists.

" Every flea market has its scam artists and Porta Portese is no exception. When you see a number of men, usually five, huddled around a small portable

table, approach with caution unless you want to be lured into their trap. Their game is '*Carta vince, carta perde*', 'Now you see it, now you don't'. It's a street hustler's classic that's been around for centuries. This is what happens. The most dexterous of the group shows the ace of spades to the public, mixes it into the other two cards, shuffles and lays them face down on the table inviting you to bet. Only the accomplices – who take their roles so earnestly that they could surely find honest employment as extras at Cinecittà – take part in the first betting. They have already decided between themselves who'll win so that when he wins again whoever is watching inevitably thinks to himself (it's usually men who fall for this one) that it's child's play. And here things get complicated. Let's say the apparently easy movement of the cards caught your eye and you're convinced you can win. You move towards the table and the winner invites you to take his place, saying it's easy and waving a crisp €100 note in your face. *Va bene*, so you watch the movements of the cards and bet on the ace of spades. Guess what? You win, not once but twice. Beginner's luck? No way. Things get heavier as the stooges urge you to bet again and to double the stake. Feeling lucky you do, only this time the movement isn't so obvious and you lose track of the ace. Not convinced, you bet again, and once more you lose. At this point you've lost more money than you started with. You'd like to try and win your money back but the band push you away, close up the table and move away to hoodwink new victims. The only protection you have against them is to not become involved.

GIFT-SHOPPING

A charming city stroll

In an unfamiliar city it's always satisfying to know where you can buy something special at a reasonable price, and even more so if you can enjoy some of Rome's most charming backstreets on your way. This walking tour takes you southwest of Rome's main shopping spine, Via del Corso, and into a network of sidestreets dotted with smaller, independent boutiques.

Begin at Largo di Torre Argentina, where the Roman ruins at the centre of this congested square provide shelter for stray cats (see page 267 in 'La Bella Figura' chapter). Concealed in a courtyard behind a wild wisteria vine at 7 Via dei Barbieri, a narrow street more or less opposite the point where trams park, is Spazio Sette[1] (Space 7). This designer houseware shop is blessed with ceiling frescoes by the Giminiani brothers and is a mecca for those seeking gifts to bear home, with its array of pleasing practical gadgets, modern furniture and objets d'art.

Return to the square, or *largo*, and to the right of the Feltrinelli[2] bookshop (which in addition to its shelves of tomes also sells DVDs, unusual magazines, maps, posters and creative T-shirts), turn left down Via dei Cestari, then right along Via Pigna and through the small square to Via del

Gesù. This sunless street is home to Materie,[3] which sells cutting-edge jewellery and accessories such as scarves and bags sourced from a pool of local artisans. Next door, Ditta G Poggi[4] has been providing an enticing range of artists' materials since 1825.

The end of Via del Gesù brings you to Via del Piè di Marmo (Street of the Marble Foot) where a handful of eyecatching boutiques vie for attention with ecclesiastical haute couture. This is the Savile Row of Vatican fashion. None sells to the public but the mannequins, respectably clad in scarlet silk gowns with a purple sash and a *zucchetto* (skullcap), make a striking change from your average window display.

Beyond the ruby curtains and quaint doorbell at nos. 21–22 is a local landmark, the Confetteria Moriondo e Gariglio.[5] Since 1886 this old-fashioned sweet shop perfumed by the warm scent of chocolate has been making home-made pralines, chocolates and jellied fruits for sweet-toothed royalty and devoted locals alike. Sculpted chocolates are made on commission.

Via del Piè di Marmo leads to Piazza della Minerva. On the far side of the piazza at 34 Via di San Chiara, opposite the church, is the tiny Gammarelli shop which acts as the pope's personal tailor. Beyond Piazza della Minerva is the Emperor Hadrian's second-century Pantheon, which contains the tombs of Raphael and the first king of united Italy, Vittorio Emanuele II. The pop artist Roy Lichtenstein once said the Romans needed a giant cork to plug the circular hole (9 metres in diameter) at the centre of the dome. To the right of the Pantheon as you face it is the Grace Gallery,[6] where the American owner, Nancy Robinson, sells her stunning photographs of Italy – she first settled in Sorrento but was seduced by Rome.

The Pantheon's magnificent portico overlooks Piazza della Rotonda, and in the far left-hand corner of the square Via della Rosetta leads into Via della Maddalena, where the neighbourhood *ferramenta*, or ironmonger's, is a workaday shop offering classic cafetieres, clocks, bric-a-brac and copies of Ancient Roman earthenware.

A swift stroll north along Via Campo Marzio will bring you to Campo Marzio Penne,[7] a tiny shop selling handmade writing materials produced in its workshop, including antique-style fountain pens, wax seals and leather-bound notebooks.

If you feel the need to refuel or write a few postcards, drop into Vic's[8] on Vicolo della Toretta, where an inspired salad with a glass of wine costs from about €10.

Return to Via della Maddalena turning right when you reach Via delle Coppelle, along which the sparsely decorated Giu & Ga[9] offers a vast spread of designer clothes at sensible prices. New deliveries arrive on Tuesdays and Fridays.

Continue through Piazza Sant'Agostino until you reach the busy Corso del Rinascimento, the site of the family-owned Ai Monasteri,[10] a sort of holy deli that sells the fruits of Italy's monastic orders. Among its sacred produce you will find liqueurs, preserves, perfume and traditional remedies, including an elixir for longevity.

Cross the road to join the ambling streams of tourists in Piazza Navona. De Sanctis, at nos. 82–84, has been selling an extensive range of decorative ceramics from various regions of Italy for over a century. Beyond the western side of the piazza, Via del Governo Vecchio has a host of eclectic boutiques and fancy second-hand shops worth a rummage.

Too Much,[11] on Via Santa Maria dell'Anima, lives up to its name with two floors of kitsch gizmos and household objects.

If you've come this far you should have found a gift for even the most challenging recipient, and from an outdoor table at the nearby Bar della Pace,[12] on the corner of Piazza Santa Maria della Pace, you can reflect on the day's shopping over a *cappuccino* or a glass of *prosecco* at one of Rome's trendiest old haunts.

1 SPAZIO SETTE, 7 Via dei Barbieri, 06 6830 7139, open daily, except Mon am & Sun.
2 FELTRINELLI, 5a Largo di Torre Argentina, 06 6880 3248, open daily until 8pm.
3 MATERIE, 73 Via del Gesù.
4 DITTA G POGGI, 74–75 Via del Gesù, 06 678 4477, closed Sun.
5 CONFETTERIA MORIONDO E GARIGLIO, 21–22 Via del Piè di Marmo, 06 699 0856.
6 GRACE GALLERY, 3 Via della Rotonda, 06 9760 3377, www.gracegallery.com, open 10am–7pm daily.
7 CAMPO MARZIO PENNE, 41 Via Campo Marzio, 06 361 0309.
8 VIC'S, 60 Vicolo della Toretta, 06 687 1445, closed Sun.
9 GIU & GA, 16 Via delle Coppelle, 06 6889 2865, open daily until 8pm.
10 AI MONASTERI, 72 Corso del Rinascimento, 06 6880 2783, open daily, except Thurs pm and Sun.
11 TOO MUCH, 29 Via Santa Maria dell'Anima, 06 6830 1187, open noon–midnight daily.
12 BAR DELLA PACE, 3–7 Via della Pace, 06 686 1216, open 9am–2am Tues to Sun, 3pm–2am Mon.

CHRISTIE'S
AUCTIONS

Old Masters for sale

To add a dash of drama to your shopping, international auctioneers Christie's[1] holds biannual sales, for a few days in spring (May/June) and late autumn (November/early December) at its headquarters in Rome.

While an old master might be out of your league, the office is well worth a visit in its own right. Housed in the Renaissance Palazzo Massimo Lancellotti, at the far end of Piazza Navona, the stunning view from its reception room takes in such Baroque masterpieces as Bernini's Fontana dei Quattro Fiumi and Borromini's church of Sant'Agnese. Equally impressive is the main room of the *piano nobile* (first floor) which is covered with the remains of colourful sixteenth-century frescoes celebrating the appointment of the original owner's nephew as Archbishop of Monreale. Used as a theatre in the eighteenth century, this room has been the stage for auctions since Christie's Rome office (opened in 1958) moved here in 1975.

Unlike Christie's sales rooms at King Street, St James's, London, the Rome office covers the auction room walls with the official lots, adding a more intimate dimension to the sale. Inspecting the lots on preview days prior to a sale is like visiting a private museum, as goods on view often include jewellery, silver, icons, watches, paintings, sculptures, books, manuscripts and prints. At a recent 'Old Master Drawings and Paintings' auction some 190 lots brought in just over €2.5 million.

The auction catalogues and the bidding processes are entirely in Italian, due to the majority of native clients present, but a number of Christie's staff are multi-lingual and therefore used to assisting non-Italian clients during the auction. Since the lira was replaced by the euro it's become much easier to keep track of prices.

Images of the objets d'art are beamed on to TV screens around the room, creating the feeling you are on an upmarket live-TV shopping channel. Suitably the auctioneer exudes the charisma and control of a TV host over the well-tailored bidders. He works at up to eighty lots per hour.

On this occasion, despite the fact that the Old Master market is drying up in terms of quality and quantity, an early-fifteenth-century *sacra conversazione* polyptych prompts an exciting bidding war, finally selling for €480,000 – a coup for the auction house. The sale of Bernardo Strozzi's beautiful interpretation of *St John the Baptist* (*c*.1619) for €125,000 also turns several heads in the room. I'm told that on another occasion the tension was palpable when bidding was delayed due to an Italian World Cup game shifting into extra time.

The current vogue is for big-name drawings. 'Clearly the relatively low prices of drawings combined with their uniqueness, spontaneity and lightness in comparison to oil paintings have gained appeal,' I am told by Aurelia Brandt, who is the Head of the Old Master Drawings and Paintings Department for Italy.

Although exceedingly complicated laws physically bind much 'great' Italian art to the *Bel Paese*, a lot of exceptional pieces do slip through the bureaucratic net and on to the international art market. For example, in 1998 Christie's attained the official record for the most expensive piece of jewellery ever sold in Italy when a *c.*1950 Bulgari white and coloured diamond brooch fetched just over two billion lire (about €1 million).

1   CHRISTIE'S ROME, Palazzo Massimo Lancellotti, 114 Piazza Navona, 06 686 3333, www.christies.com, open 9am–1pm & 2pm–6pm Mon to Fri.

ITALICA BOOKS

A bibliophile's haven

Way back in the 1990s, whenever I ran out of reading material I would drop by an apartment just off Campo de' Fiori from which an American woman, Louise McDermott, ran Italica Books,[1] selling books, in English, on Italy. On winter afternoons she would serve hot drinks and brownies while you browsed nineteenth-century first editions of travelogues or some light reading from the *bella Italia* school of literature. The visits soothed my occasional pangs for home and its cups of tea and libraries.

McDermott, now in her sixties, began her collection in 1986 when she acquired a small amount of stock from a departing expat. Then, each summer she would set off to England with her husband, Michael – they met beneath Bernini's *baldacchino* (canopy) in St Peter's – on what they called 'the hunt'. This meant scouring the second-hand bookshops of the Home Counties for bargains with an Italian slant. The haul would then be shipped back to Rome and offered at weekly coffee mornings to its residents and visitors.

After Michael passed away in 2001 McDermott found it too expensive to stay on in the *centro storico* and moved, along with her 1,700 books, to her country bolthole

in Calcata, a medieval hilltop village 50km (30 miles)
north of Rome. At first I thought how inconvenient it was;
then I made the one-hour trip. It was well worth it, not just
for the books, but also for the village's serenity and breathtaking natural beauty so close to the perpetual hullabaloo
of Rome.

Calcata is a dramatic place. It sits tightly coiled on a
slice of volcanic rock, commanding sweeping views of the
wooded valley that surrounds it. Not surprisingly its
cracked pebbled pathways and rustic rooftops make it a
popular location for film directors and Roman weekenders.
The hamlet has an otherworldly atmosphere, with its arts
and crafts shops and vegetarian-friendly foodstops. When I
visited on a weekday, a couple of doped peace-punks and
some sleepy cats and dogs were the sole presence in the
village's small piazza.

I arrived at an arched wooden door at the end of an
alley carrying a fistful of bursting figs scrumped from the
roadside trees. Beyond the silver plaque inscribed with
'Italica Books', was a homely cottage, built on several
levels, with a vast fireplace.

Once inside McDermott put on the reality specs for
me. What with burglaries, flooding in the medieval houses,
bickering hippies and a local pastor fond of *vino*, the place is
not the peaceful retreat one might at first suppose. She
thinks that Calcata has become pretentious, full of 'phoney
artists' and weekend restaurants catering for weekend
crowds. She has also discovered that the local church
apparently keeps a relic of the holy foreskin, preserved
following Christ's ritual circumcision and encased in a ruby
and emerald studded box — in homage, Calcata's annual
festival is celebrated on 1 January, the day of circumcision.

McDermott's books on Italy, many rare and out-of-print, are displayed around the living room, shelved according to regions. It's a bookish Italophile's dream. There are multiple copies of timeless reads such as H V Morton's *The Waters of Rome*, Augustus Hare's *Walks in Rome*, published in 1875 when the modern capital was but an infant, and Baedeker's guides from the turn of the century to the Fascist years, offering a window on to the Italy often recreated by Merchant and Ivory and a fascinating point of comparative reference.

'I try to keep my stock focused to my 400 regular customers' needs so I don't have to prune away dead wood,' says McDermott. Her greatest coup to date was Edward Lear's *Journals of a Landscape Painter in Southern Calabria*, a first edition published in 1852. She also briefly possessed a first edition of H Swinburne's *Travels in the Two Sicilies*, published in 1783–5.

It's very satisfying to handle some of the older books – to touch their stone-hard marbled covers, ridged spines and gilt-embossed titles – and marvel at their own history. Inside the cover of one that I carefully open there is a folded map of Rome printed on linen. In our age of the imperious mega-bookstore and the World Wide Web, this seems a far more rewarding way to buy a book. Although, since Italica Books moved out of Rome, some of its business has shifted to the Internet where it has buyers from Europe and America.

McDermott sources new books through a network of collectors, and occasionally she is tipped off about a foreigner leaving Italy. She recently bought the cream of a collection belonging to an 85-year-old woman who had grown tired of Rome and was moving to Istanbul.

For McDermott, who had previously worked as a librarian, it is a business that combines her love of Italy and books. She used to sleep with a book in her arms even before she could read, and planning which books to pack was always the most important aspect of organising any trip. As for Rome, she was seduced by its 'colour, the Italian sense of fairness, people's engagement in life, and their beautiful manners.'

From the quiet loftiness of Calcata she reflects on life in the historic centre long before Campo de' Fiori became the rowdy playground it is today. It's a view echoed by many people of her generation.

> In the Sixties and Seventies there was still a sense of living in a parish. It was the days before Ikea, and all the shops or people you might have needed lived on the one street. It took us more than a year to get a phone installed, but in the interim the shop opposite would take our calls and yell messages across the street. Until the early Nineties the Vineria used to be the only bar in the Campo, then they started handing out numerous licences and the place has become unliveable.

In the relative peace of Italica Books's present home McDermott is happy to have left Rome behind. She can visit the Eternal City when she chooses – as an OAP she can buy a discounted monthly travel pass and has free access to Rome's museums and galleries. Besides, rather than use the local post office she prefers to take the train into Rome to send orders abroad care of the famously efficient Vatican Post. 'Not only is it much faster, it's less expensive than the Roman postal service,' she says.

As I leave Calcata a shopkeeper is cursing a hippy and his stray dog who have wandered into his premises. His shouts break the hushed spell of siesta. Under my arm I have two more books than I can really afford. You just can't have a passion for both the written word and Italy and find nothing of interest at Italica Books.

1   ITALICA BOOKS, 33 Via della Pietà, 01030 Calcata, 07 6158 9047, www.italicabooks.com. Visit the website to find out when book sales and coffee mornings take place.

" Whoever left a copy of *I, Claudius* on the steps of the senate building in the Roman Forum had clearly thought about its readership. Rome has become the unlikely *caput mundi* of a mystery literary craze called BookCrossing, which ambitiously aims to 'turn the whole world into a library'. In the words of Ron Hornbaker, its American founder, it aims 'to create a continuous literary dialogue between people who love to share what they've read'.

It works like this: when a book is registered at the BookCrossing website (www.bookcrossing.com) it is allocated a unique book code; you write the code, and a message if you want, in the inside cover and leave the book on a park bench, a train, in a café or wherever you like. Whoever finds or 'catches' the book can then inform you, via the website, where and how it was found and what he or she thought of it, before liberating it again on its journey towards its unknown next reader.

There is no shortage of history-rich locations to deposit books in Rome. For instance, a copy of Marcus Aurelius's *Meditations* was left on the plinth of his statue on the Campidoglio; Robert Louis Stevenson's *Treasure Island* was left in a waiting room at Termini Station; and Pier Paolo Pasolini's *A Violent Life* was left in the Bar da Vezio, a shrine to Communism, in the Ghetto. Meanwhile, a 27-year-old female BookCrosser from Lazio received some spirited feedback when an elderly gentleman found a collection of Pope John Paul II's poems that she'd left on a pew in Santa Maria della Pace.

For others it's a voyeuristic sport. They plant a book in a coffee shop, perhaps with an inflammatory title or cover, and then settle down to watch how browsers react to it and who takes it away, logging on later to check for any response.

Although the sneaky anonymity of BookCrossing is part of its appeal to many members, BookCrossers convene in a restaurant or bookshop cafe, such as Bibli in Trastevere (see page 76 in the 'Trastevere Trail' chapter), on the evening of the second Tuesday of every month. The rendezvous is organised via www.meetup.com, a website that facilitates meetings for virtual communities. With the biggest monthly meetup group in the world, book fever is spreading across the seven hills of Rome.

Locals find it refreshing to have discovered a website that genuinely fosters goodwill and enlightenment with a dash of serendipity. 'Romans don't have local public libraries and we watch a lot of television,' a BookCrosser tells me. 'It's nice to share the written word, especially in such a romantic way.'

In search of feedback, the first time I tried leaving a book in my local bar, the waiter came chasing after me waving my dog-eared copy of Alberto Moravia's *Roman Tales*. Undeterred, I left a copy of Henry

James's *Daisy Miller* in a niche inside the Colosseum, where some of the novel's action takes place. A week later a message popped up on my screen saying: 'Finding this book made my day. *Grazie.*'

MUSEUMS MONUMENTS AND GARDENS

IL
VITTORIANO

The pomp and the glory

The Victor Emmanuel II monument[1] has been called a lot of things. The 'Wedding Cake' and 'Mussolini's Typewriter' are two of its more pleasant nicknames. Call it what you will, we can no longer grumble about this architectural leviathan as a waste of space. In the past the doors of this monument to the Italian royal family have been open only to select 'friends' of the city, such as the director Peter Greenaway who set part of his film *The Belly of an Architect* (1987) in its innards. Now, finally, the 'Altar of the Homeland' or 'Il Vittoriano', as it is otherwise officially known, is open to the public. And because of its XXL-size and its *centralissimo* location between the Colosseum and the Pantheon, tourists, Romans and Italians are flooding in. The fact that it is free and has six entrance points helps, too.

Romans have begun to revise their views since having access to the object they pilloried. Gone are the petitions to deport it to EUR, now that architects and historians are talking about the Vittoriano as the 'eighth hill of Rome', and as 'a lay basilica' that acts as a counterpoint to St Peter's and symbolises a new and diverse Italy. Its architect, Giuseppe Sacconi, who dedicated most of his working life to the building between 1883 and 1911, would be pleased to know that his opus is finally being seen and used in a new light.

Still, it is a building that puzzles onlookers. Why on earth did Rome, a city for whom the Industrial Revolution was a non-event, build an industrial scale monument? What's more, why serve up faux classicism in American portions? Unquestionably, its scale and pallor jar with original classical order even in its ruinous state. In Washington, Paris and Berlin neo-classicism looks grand, in Rome it looks kitsch.

And yet looked at closely its individual elements, its winged statues, calcified friezes and stunning Art Nouveau mosaics are awesome. There's something quite 'antique Roman' about standing on the dizzying terrace of this film-set-like building; it is here that you can best envisage being emperor, and proclaiming your vision to the citizens of Rome below – as Mussolini once did from the balcony on Palazzo Venezia across the piazza.

In fact, Il Duce envisaged a whole new series of buildings to line the adjacent Via dei Fori Imperiali, including one with a plain concave futuristic façade with only a high, narrow platform jutting out like a diving board, from which he might give his victory speeches. These designs of egomania would have seriously changed the landscape of this part of Rome. A process that had already been set in motion when Sacconi's grandiose design, inspired by the altar of Pergamon, was chosen from among 98 entries and the foundation stone of the Vittoriano was laid in 1885. Medieval and Renaissance buildings were destroyed to make way, including the ancient monastery of Ara Coeli, a Franciscan guest house and, together with a large number of private houses, the tower of Paul II. On the plus side, fossilised remains of a prehistoric elephant were found along with sections of the ancient Servian city walls.

Ironically, for such an indelible monument, the royal family's reign was brief. Italy's first king, Vittorio Emanuele II, to whom the Vittoriano is dedicated, died in 1878, shortly after the monument was begun. By 1946, King Umberto II, heir to the original monarch, was banished from Italy for his wartime support of Mussolini. He died in exile in 1983. Only in 2002 was it agreed by the Italian government that his descendants could return.

Umberto's son, also named Vittorio Emanuele, was just a young boy when his father was exiled. With only a few vague memories of Rome and Naples, he has lived most of his life in Geneva and at Cavallo, in Corsica, where in August 1978 during an argument at a port he allegedly fired a harpoon gun killing a German tourist, Dirk Hamer. The case went to court in France, but 'Viktor', as he is known in the pages of Europe's celebrity photo magazines, was cleared.

When the royals finally set foot on Italian soil, on a visit to Rome in December 2002, there were anti-monarchist protests and none of the pomp and ceremony epitomised by the bombastic Vittoriano. After nearly sixty years of absence, revisiting the capital from which, had fate decreed, he might once have ruled, must have been an extraordinary experience for Viktor, and for his thirty-year-old son, Emanuele Filiberto, who had never before been to Italy.

Italians, on the whole, are quite indifferent about the royals' return. Some academics are against it on the basis that important documents and archives relating to the Savoy family, to which the royals belong, and twentieth-century Italian history have gone missing or are being withheld.

Of course, the Vittoriano is as much about the unification of Italy as it is a memorial to a short-lived monarchy.
Despite its obdurate solidity and pride-of-place location in
a city that was once *caput mundi* ('head of the world')
politically, as a symbol of nationality, it's a building that
defies credence. With the exception of when Italy plays
international football, Italians struggle to find a common
national voice. Although many Italians will talk about their
capital in superlatives, the Milanese have a saying that the
best view of Rome is the one in the wing mirror as they
drive back to the north along the A1 *autostrada*.

According to locals the best view in Rome is from the
Vittoriano, not only because of the extensive panorama
from the terrace, but because these are the only views in the
city not marred by the monument itself. Rome is always
beautiful from a vantage point – it quite simply has the
colours, shapes and dimensions to be so. To the south side
you can almost see what pasta sauce the wealthy inhabitants
of the Ghetto are having for lunch on their idyllic, plant-
strewn roof gardens that sprout like carrot tops from the
cluster of buildings below. The view of the Pantheon's
upturned pudding-bowl roof is unique. The only blight to
the view is aural not visual; the rising roar of the traffic that
swamps Piazza Venezia below is deafening.

Walking in the shaded path of the terrace behind the
Vittoriano gives you an idea of its vast scale as well as what
was knocked down to make way for the monument. You are
slap-bang in the middle of Rome and yet it's like being in a
quiet, marbled hill-top town of Umbria.

Above the terrace, the view from the top-floor
colonnade beyond the Herculean Corinthian columns is
quite special. It's like being inside a trompe l'oeil landscape

looking out. Quite rightly it was being used for a magazine fashion shoot when I ascended its heights; the tourists were transfixed by the lean model's beauty and the view stretching a mile down the Via del Corso between her legs.

From the top floor you can truly appreciate the dimensions of the king's equestrian statue. At 10 metres long – and with a moustache that would turn many Italian men green with envy – it dwarfs the gilded bronze equestrian statue of Marcus Aurelius that crowns the Capitoline below. Apparently on completion of the casting work on the horse's belly, a lunch was served inside the statue to 21 Roman VIPs in complete comfort. The horse looks ready to leap off and gallop down the dark and narrow length of the Corso, just like in one of the wild riderless horse races inaugurated by Paul II in 1466 that gave the street its name.

The monument sits on the fringe of the Roman Forum, and beneath it is a maze of Roman and medieval tunnels and, apparently, an air-raid shelter built in 1940. To its side are *insulae*, or Roman tenements, discovered in 1927.

Inside the spacious bowels of the Vittoriano there's a lot of direly translated guff about Italy badly needing a national monument. The pamphlet in English makes the schoolboy mistake of referring throughout to the period of nineteenth-century nationalism that culminated in the unification of Italy in 1870 as the 'Renaissance' and not correctly as the Risorgimento.

The monument's airy, vaulted stairwells and corridors seem like those of a major museum stripped of its art, though attempts have been made to fill the spaces. Temporary art exhibitions are now hosted in the Brasini Wing – the first to open displayed pictures by Sean Connery's wife. There's a Hall of Flags (a general-knowledge favourite with young ones) but most interesting of all is the re-opened Central Museum of the Risorgimento.[2]

There is a solemn air to this collection, set in a semi-annular gallery lined with busts of the architects of the Risorgimento. But the Garibaldi memorabilia steals the show: primary sources include a neat leather boot complete with bullet hole where Garibaldi was shot in battle at Aspromonte. Also on display is a fragment of the bullet and his chipped leg bone, with the scene of Garibaldi heroically receiving treatment depicted in a painting above. There is one of the famous red shirts that Garibaldi's soldiers wore — which, with its green trim, looks to me like a cross between a pyjama top and a New Romantic outfit. Finally, the makeshift stretcher made from ropes and planks of wood manages to bring home the ghastly realities of the nineteenth century's brand of warfare just as well as the more fearsome torpedos on display.

Because of its sheer bulk the Vittoriano is a great orientation marker. It also makes a roomy playground for the kids marvelling at the uniformed officers guarding the Tomb of the Unknown Soldier and its memorial, the Eternal Flame.

1 COMPLESSO DEL VITTORIANO, Via San Pietro in Carcere, 06 699 1718, open 9.30am–4.30pm daily. The museums and exhibition space are open until later.

2 MUSEO CENTRALE DEL RISORGIMENTO, 06 678 0664, open 10am–6pm daily, except Mon, admission free.

GALLERIA DORIA PAMPHILJ

A prince's private art collection

After visiting one of Rome's, indeed the world's, finest private art collections at the Galleria Doria Pamphilj,[1] many women are intrigued to know who the man is behind the silky tones of the audio commentary. Like Pope Innocent X, whose portrait by Velázquez is one of the gallery's highlights, the smoothly spoken art commentator is one of the family. Don Jonathan is a modern-day prince, the adopted son – plucked from an English orphanage at the age of two by the Princess Doria Pamphilj – and joint heir, along with his sister, of the Doria Pamphilj fortunes.

My rendezvous with a real prince in Rome was confirmed by a message handed to me by the concierge at the Hotel de Russie: '*Egregio Sig. Wyke, Il principe Doria La aspetterà . . .*' The words seemed to weigh heavy with formality. Now I would meet the Prince, who opens his home to the public year round, to gain a glimpse behind the scenes of the art gallery experience.

With seven entrances to Palazzo Doria Pamphilj, the odds were stacked against me finding the one staffed by the porter. After attempts at two gates I found the diminutive doorman with his equally small wife in one of those old fashioned doorkeeper's offices not much bigger than a confession box. After a series of phone calls I was ushered in through a gate and met in the courtyard by the Prince's yapping dogs. A maid, perhaps from Eastern Europe, escorted me up two flights of stairs into a grand hall with marble floors and paintings, leading into an antechamber with softer lights and a rich museum-like décor. It was a curiously dated experience, like walking through a scene from a Visconti film.

I'd imagined being introduced to the Prince in the same stodgy, public fashion that Gregory Peck was presented to the princess at the end of *Roman Holiday*. As it happened, the Prince was waiting for me alone in his office where an open fire glowed below silk panels by Piranesi. A bottle of white wine sat chilling in a bucket. The Prince served me a glass himself. Where was the butler, I wondered?

The wine had been brought over at the last minute on the back of a scooter, from a family cellar in the Ghetto. Don Jonathan told me, 'All my life I've bought my wine from this wonderful Roman family, they are people of immense culture. Their brash, loud accents remind me of London's Eastenders in some ways; they are very witty. Their greatest quality is not taking themselves too seriously.'

Dressed in a suit and designer glasses, the Prince looked exactly how he sounded on his audio art commentaries, like a tidy presenter of an art history documentary. He was relaxed – just back from a trip with friends to Australia and New Zealand – and spoke in pristine English that he'd acquired at Downside public school in England.

No sooner has he responded uneasily to my first question, 'How does it feel to be heir to a noble Roman family?', than he exercises his royal prerogative by refusing

to answer any of the stacks of questions that I have ready for
him about his private life. 'Growing up among such privilege
for me was completely normal. I've been living in an ivory
tower all my life. Certainly nothing is taken for granted.'

We persevere with talk about Rome and the gallery.
What with the Prince's busy winter-travel schedule – he
says he would go mad if he didn't manage to get away from
central Rome and the weighty responsibility of the Doria
estate – we had exchanged several letters before we finally
met. He confesses:

> It would have been far easier if we had just met
> buying *zucchini* at the market and went for a coffee.
> Rome is still a very informal and spontaneous capital
> and for me that's everything. I love to get lost in its
> backstreets. One of the great luxuries of Rome is its
> small village atmosphere. You can bump into friends
> and arrange things on the spot. It's something they
> don't have in Milan and London.

He recalls how inert Rome used to be during the
summertime when he was growing up. He feels that
the Estate Romana (Roman Summer) programme has
changed that: 'The city is opening up; important artists are
exhibiting here and façades of great buildings are being
restored. Although the city has made some efforts to use
environmentally friendly transport, Rome is really filthy;
you can feel the pollution from the scooters when it's
really hot.' Proof of the pudding is his own Palazzo's
blackened façade on Via del Corso which was cleaned
fewer than fifteen years ago.

As his own contribution to Rome's recent renaissance, Jonathan has overseen the restoration and re-hanging

of the Doria Pamphilj Gallery. In doing so he has continued in the tradition of his parents by allowing people to enjoy his family's extraordinary collection of art. The gallery's historic rooms include works by Raphael, Caravaggio, Titian and Guido Reni. He says:

> It's not a criticism of other families in Europe, but there are too many important paintings here to keep it closed. The great thing that my parents taught me is that we are really just the custodians for the next generations. That's the deal.
>
> Yes, it's a beautiful palazzo, but it's also a responsibility. Everything happens, from the sublime to the ridiculous; from the public aspect of my life, to old ladies locking themselves in the lavatory. I can't leave the office without being grabbed by the coat tails. A sense of humour is terribly important.

The palace has 150 apartments ranging from two to twenty rooms. How does he select his tenants? 'It's our house so we can choose. In fact lots of friends live here, which is fun.'

As if on cue, we are interrupted by a young man in a silk dressing gown who seems to have come through the wrong door – an easy mistake in such a huge palace. It's a real *Talented Mr Ripley* moment – he is promptly but politely dismissed by the Prince. 'I've grown up with groups of tourists in my house,' he says.

Despite what the tabloids call his 'rags to riches' life story, referring to his early childhood spent in an orphanage, Jonathan says he would have chosen an art history career regardless of his background. Stood in the palazzo's ballroom with its burnished mirrors and shimmering chandeliers, he talks over the background strains of Handel – the composer was a guest here on his first visit to Rome. 'When I was a child, the state rooms were abandoned. My sister and I would get into trouble for roller-skating over the floors. With its reopening I feel that the palace has been brought back to life.'

When I refer to his regal, radio-presenter voice that the housewives crave, he says, 'I know, people say it's very soothing. I sound like I should be hosting a late-night jazz programme.' Right now, though, the Prince is too busy to diversify into a second career as a DJ.

1   GALLERIA DORIA PAMPHILJ, 2 Piazza del Collegio Romano, 06 679 7323, www.doriapamphilj.it, open 10am–5pm daily, except Thurs, €8.

WAXWORKS
MUSEUM

Virtual reality

Since 1958 the prestigious Colonna family has rented a small section of their grand palazzo in Piazza Santi Apostoli to the Canini family. The Caninis do not live there; rather the place is inhabited by about fifty waxwork characters from the realms of history, myth and celebrity. For many years the rooms were rented at a favourable rate, but in 2000 the young Prince Colonna upped the charge to keep it more in line with market values (though I suspect that given its tremendous central location it is still a bit of a steal).

The Museo delle Cere[1] (Waxworks Museum) was opened in 1958 after Fernando Canini was inspired by a visit to the famous waxworks museums in London and Paris. During my guided tour his grandson, the current owner and also named Fernando, refers frequently to Madame Tussaud's as his personal Mecca. He has never been to London's leading tourist attraction and dreams of being able to hire the sort of sculptors who can shape Kylie Minogue's derrière to such a likeness, and of having the funds to add the likes of Michael Schumacher and Eros Ramazotti to this somewhat random collection of heroes.

Ingenuously, Canini complains that the state is not interested in his plans to renovate the museum. But his plans

are patchy and he seems to lack conviction. Although he has
laid a new floor, he might have been better advised to
concentrate on the attractions themselves. Some of the
waxworks – which are just busts and hands on clothed
wooden frames – are frayed and difficult to recognise.

Dante, who stands in a group that includes Abraham
Lincoln, has the longest ski-slope nose you've ever seen
outside of fiction. Napoleon is the height he would have
liked to have been and would easily scare birds away. When
I mention this, Canini is at first defensive and then gives a
shrug of *menofreghismo* (an ageing Roman syndrome of not
giving a damn). Other models have dirty collars and dusty
lapels where the pollution seeps in through the windows.

Corridors lead to dim dead-ends lined with superfluous
junk – for instance, toy dinosaurs on their last legs and cheap
reconstructions of a few execution tools. Amazingly, the only
two famous women in the entire collection are figments of
male artists' imaginations: Leonardo da Vinci's Mona Lisa and
Charles Perrault's Sleeping Beauty. None the less, there
remains a certain cranky, olde-worlde charm to the place. And
I can guarantee you two things: no queues and a laugh.

The exhibition plunges you straight into a meeting of
Mussolini's Grand Fascist council in 1943, as it sat to
deliberate its defeat by the Allies. It's a dark and ominous
gathering. The faces have a translucent, plastic look like spoof
masks with sculpted hair. So similar are some of the
representatives that they might well have come from the
same mould. Local resident Silvio Berlusconi with his round,
rubbery perma-tan face would fit in smoothly. A real-life
member of staff is dropping off to sleep in the corner to the
crackling sounds of a transistor radio playing *Red, Red Wine* –
not exactly the melodramatic strains of a Fascist anthem.

And just for the record, the paintings on the wall, of presumably classical scenes, are the worst I've seen in Rome.

By the time we reach the Musicians and Artists display Canini is starting to look dejected. Each section has a photocopied sheet of A4 paper attached to flimsy railings on which is written 'Do Not Touch'. He leans over to re-tie Wagner's cravat which has come loose. '*Che rompe palle*' (literally, 'What ballbreakers'), he bemoans. It transpires that schoolkids have stolen Toscanini's bow tie. You get the feeling that he is fighting a losing battle.

When the latest inmates – stars of the city's two football teams, Alessandro Nesta (now playing for AC Milan) and Francesco Totti – were added to the dead-end of the corridor, one of their club ties, donated by the players, was stolen by an eager fan. Canini expresses surprise. But to me, in such a quiet and shady nook, the footballers seem like soft targets. Though you wonder how many Romans actually make it upstairs to this display, where the backdrop is a painted sheet showing the crowds at each end of the stadium minutes before kick-off in a derby match. Painted by a Lazio fan, the Roma end, the Curva Sud, remains unfinished.

A model of the Neapolitan comic Toto (renowned for his malleably expressive face) was once commissioned, but never saw the half-light of display; Canini thought the finished product didn't look sufficiently lifelike to be included. I dread to think what it looks like, then. Perhaps it's another one for the understocked chamber of horrors.

On a brighter note, a Milanese fashion campaign once borrowed a handful of the museum's wax tyrants and geniuses and clad them in designer gear for a photo shoot. Canini shows me the pictures: the staid Verdi wears a Dolce & Gabbana nylon jacket with imprints of washing powder boxes, while Napoleon, chest puffed out, sports a striped shirt and combat jacket by Versace. It could be the way forward, I suggest. Canini's eyes glimmer for a moment and then fade.

Rome's waxworks museum is the sort of place that raises rather than answers questions. Why, I wondered, is there a copy of a 1926 trade agreement between Great Britain and Italy hung in the hallway? Is that Balzac or Sherlock Holmes? Khruschev or Churchill? The Beatles or Pooh (not the bear, but an Italian four-man soft-rock supergroup)?

Although it has no chamber of horrors as such, the museum has its own stories of horror and mirth. A Spanish tourist once fainted when he saw the beating heart of Sleeping Beauty – the model has a small motor in her chest that simulates the motion of breathing. When staff revived him he fled the place screaming. On another occasion a visitor deposited a solid bodily offering on the floor to express feelings that could have been costly to show had he really been standing before the Fascist Council. Finally, a woman was petrified when she was locked in the museum one evening by lackadaisical staff. Luckily the porter from Palazzo Colonna heard her cries for help and came to the rescue.

Bizarrely, at the time I visited, there was an exhibition that claimed to be of the smallest paintings in the world. The landscapes and views of Rome measured 7mm by 7mm – the size of a small fingernail – and there was a magnifying glass attached to a cord to look at the pictures.

In a city that has spruced up its outstanding collections of art and antiquities, the waxworks museum is an anachronism, a reminder of a bygone age when Rome was still parochial and aspirant. You only have to go next door to the Colonna family collection for proof of Rome's world-beating sculpture – but clearly the sculptors' skill wasn't handed down to the waxworkers.

Canini ranks his museum as the third most important waxworks collection in Europe, but it is scarcely mentioned in tourist literature or guidebooks. And yet simply for the fact that such a place is still open, and it isn't in some kiss-me-quick seaside resort, it is worth a visit.

1   MUSEO DELLE CERE, 67 Piazza Santi Apostoli, 06 679 6482, open
    9am–8pm daily, €5.

DE CHIRICO MEMORIAL HOUSE

Home study in metaphysics

'They say Rome is the centre of the world and that Piazza di Spagna is the centre of Rome, so me and my wife would live in the centre of the centre of the world.' That was the verdict of Giorgio De Chirico, Italy's most famous twentieth-century painter, who, born in Greece in 1888, had also lived in Athens, Paris, Munich and Florence. Yet such a teeming and obviously fashionable location seemed at odds with a man whose art is mysteriously depopulated and obscure.

The shiny brass plaque and the spotless stairwell make a visit to De Chirico's fifth-floor apartment[1] in Piazza di Spagna rather like a trip to the dentist. But once inside, instead of being put into the chair and inverted, it is your reality that is turned upside down – by his art.

De Chirico's metaphysical paintings are full of 'illogical reality' – typically he juxtaposed unrelated objects to convey a sense of the unknown. Vacant piazzas play host to lone statues and are filled with ordinary things (bunches of bananas, a rubber glove, balls and books) alongside the classical debris that he would have been exposed to growing up in Greece.

On the first of the two floors, the main room is entered through sliding screen doors. It feels like you are about to step into the *This is Your Life* set. Indeed the house is a tour of De Chirico's private life, with his frozen-in-time studio and bedrooms, and the biggest collection of his paintings in the world. To visit an exhibition of sixty of his paintings in a gallery in New York or London would be a sterile experience compared to seeing the works of art here – in the very centre of Rome – where he lived, loved and worked.

Looking like the backdrop to a Martini advert from the 1970s, the flat seems rather staidly bourgeois for such a ground-breaking and imaginative artist. But it's the works of art and the minutiae that make it intriguing. The square U-shaped area contains the living room and dining room. The former has a dated television draped like a theatre stage; the only surprise is that it's not showing a news broadcast about Pasolini or the Red Brigades (apparently De Chirico would watch the TV with the sound turned off). On the drinks trolley sit half-finished bottles of vermouth and a cocktail shaker.

Both rooms are full of his paintings and sculptures. Among his trademark canvases featuring blank egg-shaped faces and scattered antiquities there are copies of Rubens and Canaletto, each with De Chirico's own deft embellishments, and, in about equal numbers, self-portraits and paintings of his wife, Isabella, usually sumptuously dressed. The dining room is decorated with delicious-looking fruit still lifes.

Upstairs is a small monastic room where during their twilight years De Chirico laid down his gargantuan frame in a tiny single bed, while his wife slept in the master bedroom across the corridor.

But regardless of what kept man and wife nocturnally separate, it is De Chirico's studio that gives you a real sense of entering his private world. At the centre of the room a work in progress is found as it was left. Natural overhead light, unique to this room, casts a streak across the easel on which the artist had barely begun a Michelangelo copy. Behind the canvas are various superstitious charms to ward off bad luck – *cornetti*, or little horns, cow bells, a tambourine and a horseshoe – and the artist's work jacket is slung across the chair where he left it.

Such is the sensation of someone having recently departed from the studio that you feel like an intruder about to be caught; that at any moment you'll hear the click of the lift and the key in the door and be face to face with his authoritative presence. It's an unlikely scenario – he died in 1978.

From his top-floor studio overlooking the rooftops of Rome, De Chirico would frequently capture with crayons and pencils the 'celestial spectacle' of the Roman sky and its inflamed sunsets. And yet he insisted that it is only the masters and not nature who can teach you to paint well: 'Only after copying a drawing of a tree hundreds of times can you copy a real tree with confidence.'

That De Chirico himself was a master is illustrated by the number of great painters who have expressed a debt to him. Two of the most eminent were Max Ernst and Salvador Dali. While the Surrealists were striving to find new abstract forms to highlight the escalating changes to man and his condition in the first half of the twentieth century, art historians record De Chirico as 'a painter of eternity' who stuck to the outward appearances of reality in his quest to capture on canvas the universality of being. And where better to seek the big picture than at the centre of the Eternal City?

Note: for those in need of an antidote to an overdose of classical and Renaissance art, more De Chirico can be found at the Galleria Nazionale d'Arte Moderna e Contemporanea[2] in the Villa Borghese. The neoclassical palazzo also houses a time-trip tea room, the Caffè delle Arti.

1 CASA MUSEO DI DE CHIRICO, 31 Piazza di Spagna, 06 679 6546, open 10am–1pm Tues to Sat and the first Sun of the month, €5. Booking is essential.
2 GALLERIA NAZIONALE D'ARTE MODERNA E CONTEMPORANEA, 131 Viale delle Belle Arti, 06 322 981, open 8.30am–7.30pm Tues to Sun, €6.50.

THE
PROTESTANT
CEMETERY

A Roman plot

As you approach the Protestant Cemetery,[1] near Piramide metro station on the fringes of Testaccio, a narrow slit in the cemetery wall, covered in thick gauze, allows you a peep at Keats's grave and its verdant surrounds – the lawn is lush green, the likes of which you don't see often in Rome. One might have guessed that the site where Keats chose to be buried and about which Shelley wrote (in *Adonais*): 'It might make one in love with death, to be buried in so sweet a place' is justly serene and enchanting. After all our Romantics had an eye for mellowed beauty.

Despite his praise, Shelley's ultimate connection with the cemetery was a deeply sad one. The poet's last visit was with his wife, Mary, to bury their young son, William. He was the second child the couple had lost in the space of a year. Devastated, Shelley left Rome for good, writing to a friend that 'It is more like a sepulchre than a city, beautiful but the abode of death.' When Shelley drowned off the coast of Livorno in 1822 his ashes were brought back to Rome to rest with his son at the Protestant Cemetery. Yet when the grave was dug up there was no sign of the boy's skeleton; in its place were the bones of an adult – this remains an unsolved mystery. Not surprisingly, it was twenty years before Mary could face visiting the cemetery again. But many writers came to make the pilgrimage and although it is well and truly on Rome's tourist map, it still deserves a mention in this book.

A tug on a short chain rings a small iron bell at the entrance gate, and a gardener will come to let you in. Cross the threshold and it is like having entered a secret garden as the drone of the traffic that swings around the corner into Via Marmorata recedes and the constant chatter of crickets in the towering firs and cypress trees takes its place.

The cemetery is not vast and rambling, but it is dense. Officially known as the Cimitero Acattolico (Non-Catholic Cemetery), it hosts some four thousand 'guests' in a space about the same size as Piazza Navona. The majority are foreigners, though there is a handful of non-Catholic Italians. Its perimeter is abutted by the ancient pyramid of Caius Cestius, a funerary monument from 12 BC to the Roman governor of Egypt, flanked in turn by a Roman wall studded with scarlet flowers. Today Cestius's marbled pyramid serves to remind us of the impact of pollution. The sheltered cemetery side of this freak memento mori is much cleaner than its other three fronts besmirched by years of fumes. Still, black or white, there is nothing in the neighbouring cemetery to match its magnitude.

The first official burial took place in 1738. According to the ecclesiastical law of the time it would have been at night, and without the iconography of the crucifix or epigraphs expressing concepts such as eternity and beatitude, which were considered to be the exclusive preserve of the Holy Roman Catholic Church and were banned until 1870.

Today, as the graveyard nears capacity, it is difficult to be buried here, I am told by Luciano Salvatori, who has engraved the cemetery's tombstones for the past 25 years. He is hunched over a fresh slab of marble chipping away with a hammer and chisel beneath the shade of a tree. How does it feel to work among the spirits of the dead each day? 'It's very peaceful work, and outdoors for most of the year. I start with nothing and I create something. That's fitting work for a poets' cemetery.'

There are luminaries here, principally Shelley and Keats, but also many humble pioneers who populated the social firmament of the British in Rome. Minor royalty, dukes (of Leeds and Manchester), counts, bankers and military men, ambassadorial staff, writers, artists and TEFL teachers of their day are all united in this common ground. They lie alongside the graves of Greeks, Germans, Russians, Jews and Muslims.

Apart from the skulking cats and a couple of gardeners pottering quietly about their business, I had the place entirely to myself. Meandering among layer upon layer of graves stacked up to the back wall like theatre seats, I came across many familiar British surnames: Cartwright, Mason and Henderson, each of whom had ended up living in Rome and made the plucky decision to be buried thousands of miles from their home town.

As I continued my wander about the cemetery, I couldn't help wondering about the life of Belinda Lee whose tomb, topped by a statue of a draped torso, indicated that she was a British actress who had died aged 26 in 1961. Film biographies reveal that, born in sleepy Budleigh Salterton in Devon, she starred in 33 films in her brief seven-year career, making her debut in *The Belles of St Trinian's* in 1954 alongside George Cole and Beryl Reid, and going on to appear in historical dramas and other European films alongside many of the stellar names of Italian cinema. Frequently a cover girl on *Picturegoer* magazine, which showcased her pretty, bleached-blonde look from the school of Marilyn Monroe and Diana Dors, she developed a penchant for playing femmes fatales, and had a scandalous affair with Prince Orsini. Her promising career was cut short when she died in a car crash in California. After a low-key funeral in Hollywood, with just fifteen guests, her whirlwind life came to rest in peace on this tranquil slope in Rome.

More recently, when Gregory Corso, the bad boy of the Beat poets, was interred in front of the tomb of the rebel Romantic, Shelley, in May 2001, the British literary establishment sniffed with disapproval. The *Times Literary Supplement* said, 'It is doubtful whether his talent alone would have secured him this coveted spot' and went on to suggest that he had lied about his religion to gain the plot.

Indeed, strings were pulled. Born in New York in 1930 to Calabrian parents, Corso had dreamt of being buried close to his hero whose poetry had provided soul food to the delinquent teenager in New York's prisons. He was a long-term heroin addict and alcoholic, and was best known for such blunt verse as *Bomb*, a scathingly ironic ode to nuclear weapons written in the form of a mushroom cloud in 1958. Corso's dying wish was secured by his friend Robert Yarra who had sharp enough connections in Rome to cut through the labyrinth of red tape. The mini plot, where his ashes are interred in a bronze urn, cost a cool $5,000, some of which was raised at a benefit concert organised by friends and starring the singer Patti Smith.

But should Corso, who lived against the grain, have been given a place for eternity in the Cimitero Acattolico?

After all, he had been baptised as a Catholic and had a Catholic funeral in New York at the Lady of Pompeii, a beautiful church that wouldn't look out of place in one of Rome's squares. 'Well, it is a welcome sign of tolerance, of art triumphing over politics for once,' says Salvatori. Literary snobs can rest assured that Rome's main thorough-fare, Via del Corso, is named after the riderless horse race once held there, and not the grungy American poet.

Both Belinda Lee and Gregory Corso's graves are situated to the left of the cemetery as you enter, not far from the gardeners' workshop. A map is available at the entrance to help you locate the gravestones of famous residents.

The cemetery's Arcadian backdrop seems ideally suited to follow in the footsteps of so many of Rome's sacred sites that now host concerts and plays, as part of Rome's plentiful programmes for cultural nourishment. In 2000 the Colosseum staged Sophocles's *Oedipus Rex*, its first live performance in 1,500 years. Alas, Salvatori says, 'The commune once tried it as a site for music and poetry, but decided that it was best left for the dead.'

Against the background of deathly quiet, it is easy to become lost in a reverie of contemplation and fall victim to graveyard predators. On my midsummer visit I encountered Rome's latest invader, not the jewel-backed lizard that flashes across the gravestones, but the ferocious Tiger mosquito, a striped bug from Southeast Asia which bites during the daytime; its army took full advantage of the fresh blood in my exposed limbs. Worst of all, I felt something fleshlike brush against my back as I perched on the edge of a tomb. For a moment I thought it was the hand of the dead – and supposed, grimly, that if it was going to 'reap' me then this was as suitable a place as any. Instead it was one of the cemetery's band of plump, idling cats. You have been warned. I got up to leave, not reposed as I had hoped, but feeling rather jumpy.

Fortunately, a refreshing hand-grated ice drink with limoncello from the bar-kiosk across the road helped to bring me back to the land of the living. No doubt Keats, as he wrote in *Ode to a Nightingale*, would have approved of such a 'beaker full of the warm South'.

1   CIMITERO ACATTOLICO, 6 Via Caio Cestius, 06 574 1900, open 9am–5.30pm Tues to Sun Apr–Sept, 8am–4.30pm Tues to Sun Oct–Mar, free, but a donation is expected.

THE COMMONWEALTH WAR CEMETERY

A corner of a foreign field

Across the road from the Protestant Cemetery lies another corner of Rome that is forever England (albeit of the ageing Commonwealth variety). Nevertheless, the Commonwealth War Cemetery[1] on Via Nicola Zabaglia is very much part of the city's history. An inscription around the inside of the dome above the entrance informs us that the 426 servicemen who died in and around Rome in World War II gave 'their lives to preserve liberty and by their sacrifice restored the freedom of Italy and the ancient friendship of the Italian and British peoples.'

If the Protestant Cemetery is dense and abundant then here there is a sense of space. The pristine graves stand in rows like soldiers on parade across a lawn the size of a school playing field, flanked by the arched Aurelian wall and a row of pine trees that rise like question marks between the sad words on the headstones. What the cemeteries have in common, though, is poetry. Etched on many of the graves are popular lines from Laurence Binyon's *Ode for the Fallen*:

'At the setting of the sun/And in the morning, we will remember them' and from Rupert Brooke's *The Soldier*: 'That there's some corner of a foreign field/That is for ever England . . .'

In line with the Commonwealth War Graves Commission's founding principles the headstones are uniform (813mm in height) and each is engraved with the national emblem or the service or regimental badge. Of the buried, no distinction is made regarding military or civil rank, race or creed. Many of the graves are inscribed with simple messages from parents lamenting the fact that they will never again see the smile of their only sons. A considerable number seem to have died in their early twenties. One of which, a twenty-year-old trooper, J R Hurst of the Ontario regiment, died on 13 June 1944. The inscription on his grave reads: 'By the road to Rome/He'll rest for all eternity/A long, long, way from home.'

Rome fell to the Allies on 4 June 1944 and the construction of the cemetery began shortly afterwards. Nearly fifty thousand Commonwealth dead from the two World Wars are buried or commemorated in Italy. Compared to some of the pivotal battle sites, such as at Anzio and Cassino south of the capital, the Roman cemetery is relatively small.

Patriotism might not have been Shelley's forte, but the words of the poet laid to rest in the neighbouring cemetery are chiselled in stone on several of the headstones:

> . . . they borrow not
> Glory from those who made the world their prey;
> And he is gathered to the kings of thought

Who waged contention with their time's decay,
And of the past are all that cannot pass away.

Adonais; stanza XLVIII

1   THE COMMONWEALTH WAR CEMETERY, Via Nicola Zabaglia,
     06 855 021, open 8am–3pm Mon to Fri.

" For a lofty view of the cemetery you can climb
nearby Monte Testaccio, a shabby fenced-off area
which is itself a burial ground for heaps of broken
amphorae – ancient earthenware jars used for
shipping oil, wax, wine, honey, olives and grain. (The
gate to Monte Testaccio is at 24 Via Nicola Zabaglia;
call 06 6710 3819 for details on access.) This
artificial hill, covered in brambles and topped with an
iron cross, is home to the largest collection of Roman
pottery in the world. The base of the hill houses a
handful of popular nightclubs in what used to be
wine cellars, because apparently they stay cool even
in summertime. For clubbers with an archaeological
bent, some of the clubs display the layered shards of
amphorae behind glass walls.

VILLA
TORLONIA

At home with Il Duce

It is well known that Mussolini had a habit of leaving the lights on overnight in his 'office' overlooking the piazza at Palazzo Venezia in order to give the impression that he was hard at work mapping out the country's future. The chances are, though, that if he wasn't seeing his mistress, he was tucked up in bed with his wife Rachele (the daughter of his father's mistress), a few miles north at his beloved Villa Torlonia.[1] This two-storey neoclassical villa built in 1806 was Il Duce's residence in Rome from 1925 to 1943.

When British and American troops liberated Rome in 1944 the villa became Allied headquarters for a few years, during which time the city's present-day authorities claim the Allies wrecked the villa's interior. Post-war its imperious exterior fared little better, as weeds and graffiti spread across its façade. The building lay neglected until Rome City Council bought it in 1977 and a year later opened the grounds as a small, attractive public park. Once the most famous English landscape garden in Italy, its Moorish kiosk is just one of thirteen garden pavilions, some quite ramshackle, representing exotic parts of the world. Now as Italians become more willing to acknowledge and explore the legacy of Fascism, there are controversial plans to open a Mussolini museum when the main villa is fully restored.

Mussolini lived at Villa Torlonia with his children and mentions in letters how he would rise early to ride horses and play tennis, in the best tradition of the model Fascist male. Every day he is said to have put world affairs on hold while he returned to the villa to lunch with his family. Yet despite his rigorous self-discipline, Rachele used to complain to her husband: 'You bend forty million Italians to your will, but you are not able to make your own sons obey you.'

Of course, Mussolini was an early master of public relations. He demonstrated this by moving temporarily to Villa Torlonia in 1924 to impress the visiting Abyssinian emperor, Haile Selassie, with his private compound and showy horses. A year later he settled there for good. Conveniently for the Italian leader his landlord, Prince Torlonia, was an altruistic soul. Legend has it that the Prince kept a gold carriage ready 24 hours a day to take the famous miracle-making Santo Bambino wooden statue, kept in the church of Santa Maria in Aracoeli, to the bedsides of Rome's sick. His philanthropy extended to Mussolini who paid a nominal rent of one lira a year for his grand pile.

While Mussolini took over this minor palace, the Prince moved across the park to the now flawlessly restored Casina delle Civette (Little House of the Owls).[1] This quirky Art Nouveau folly with its majolica roof, misshapen rooms and splendid stained glass is truly an anomaly in classically inspired Rome. It would look more at home in Prague or Paris, and for the homesick expat a visit to its museum has the restorative effect of a curry washed down with a well-poured Guinness.

One highlight of Il Duce's stay at Villa Torlonia was the society wedding of his daughter, Edda, in 1929. Among the four thousand guests that filled the villa, Rachele noted that the wife of the Soviet ambassador wore more jewels than anyone else and a fur coat despite the warm Roman spring. In the same year Gandhi stayed briefly with his goat in tow, and gave his blessing to the Italian dictator. The Indian guru would no doubt approve of today's yoga classes that stretch out in the park's shade beneath the rare Californian palm trees and Lebanese cedars.

Already restored in the grounds, and a taste of things to come, is the museum at the dinky Casino dei Principi (House of the Princes), a splendid nineteenth-century rural outhouse from which Prince Torlonia would watch performances in the nearby amphitheatre. The house's fawn-coloured façade hosts fading monochrome portions of a beautiful frieze that portrayed the victory of Alexander the Great in Babylon. On display inside are fine works of art from the Torlonia family's collection including sculptures by Bartolomeo Cavaceppi and a series of bas reliefs by Antonio Canova that previously decorated the dining room of the main villa. But it is the ornate bed used by the Italian dictator that draws most people to visit. It is a novel, though slightly macabre and perverse experience to share the private space of this tyrant of recent history.

Even more compelling when Villa Torlonia is fully restored will be its original decoration. The restoration project director, Alberta Campitelli, told me the Sala di Alessandro contains frescoes by Francesco Podesti telling the story of Alexander the Great, stucco reliefs by the Danish sculptor Bertel Thorvaldsen, and a monochrome mosaic floor depicting masked dancers. The frescoes in the bathroom show scenes of Roman and Greek splendour that must have suited Mussolini's passionate drive to model

Fascism on Imperial Rome. One can imagine the barrel-chested and bald leader gloating at the images as he reclined in his bath or sat doubled over from the nervous stomach cramps from which he suffered in moments of crisis. Pin-ups painted by a GI were found in another room, and will be displayed in the new museum. Other personal effects of Mussolini may include the overcoat that he was wearing when he was shot by partisans in 1945. It was recently found in a Treasury Ministry storeroom.

Beneath the house and park lie 9km (6 miles) of Jewish catacombs dating back to the third and fourth centuries. Mussolini made part of them into a war bunker with secret tunnels to protect his family in the event of heavy bombing or a chemical attack. The thought of a Nazi ally taking shelter in Jewish graves is particularly repugnant. So too, for many Italians, is the idea of a museum dedicated to a megalomaniac who destroyed freedom and parlia-mentary government.

But the Mussolini museum in Villa Torlonia has the potential to be one of the most intriguing in Europe. 'People are fascinated by the private lives of tyrants, and the villa has some spectacular interior details,' says Campitelli. Let's hope that Il Duce-branded spin-offs – such as bottles of wine with his mugshot on the label (see the 'Vino Mussolini' chapter, page 45) – will not be available in the museum shop.

1   VILLA TORLONIA, MUSEO DELLA CASINA DELLE CIVETTE and MUSEO DEL CASINO DEI PRINCIPI, 70 Via Nomentana, 06 4425 0072, open 9am–7pm daily, except Mon, in summer, till 5pm in winter, €2.60.

ERIC HEBBORN

A fake's progress

I met the artist Eric Hebborn in 1995, just six months before his mysterious death. I had driven with a team of English footballers 65km (40 miles) east of Rome up a steeply winding road to the hilltop village of Anticoli Corrado to play an annual fixture against the local team. One character stood out from the solid, southern faces of the villagers: a solitary man with a dark, unkept beard, cream Panama hat, linen suit and cane. He approached me, raising his cane, and proudly informed me he had started the sporting fixture for which we were gathered 25 years ago. From what I remember he appeared drunk, and others dismissed him as you would a tramp in the street, but I listened as he rambled on – about how the village had been an arty retreat since a few artists from Via Margutta had married local models and come to live here – until I was called to the football pitch. Six months later I came across his obituary in a newspaper.

Hebborn was one of the twentieth century's greatest art forgers and one of the most interesting of latter-day English-speaking exiles in Rome. Born in London in 1934, a Scholarship in Engraving brought him to the British

School in Rome in 1959, just as *La Dolce Vita* (1960) was heralding a carefree era. The fledgling artist had set out walking to Rome from England in the footsteps of the Grand Tourists, but unlike the privileged travellers before him, he had no money. He carried a large army rucksack, refused offers of lifts from motorists, lived on wine and tinned sardines, and slept rough under a sheet of canvas in fields. On the road to Rome he primed himself in Italian art, spending days in the galleries of Florence and Venice where he was moved to tears by Titian, confirming his ardent preference for past masters over contemporary art.

Rome suited Hebborn. He liked its climate, its food and wine and its works by Old Masters. Hebborn also found the locals refreshingly direct. 'I loved the Romans, if for one quality alone – they hate hypocrisy.' At the dawn of the 1960s there really were fewer cars, cleaner air, and more outdoor eating and promenading in Rome than today. Among its seven hills he was able to play the wacky expat character while remaining anonymous among the vast majority of city dwellers. On his arrival he took a stroll on to the Pincio hill overlooking Rome and delighted in how the buildings seemed to absorb and reflect the light. In retrospect he noted in his autobiography, *Drawn to Trouble*:[1] 'Little did I think that one day I would visit the Villa Medici to view an exhibition of Old Masters to which I myself had made an important contribution.'

Behind the grand Lutyens's façade of the British School Hebborn enjoyed preposterous arguments with stiffnecked academics, entertaining himself by seeing how much rubbish he could talk about art and get away with unchallenged. He later claimed that he was only seriously challenged once, by the aristocratic tongue of Sir Anthony

Blunt, Surveyor of the Queen's Pictures and Director of the Courtauld Institute at the time. The unlikely pair – Hebborn had faced prejudice and snobbery for his cockney background at the exclusive Royal Academy – forged a close friendship. 'We spent the greater part of our time together drinking and discussing Old Master drawings, and I learned a great deal, not only about the drawings themselves, but what goes on in the minds of the experts who view them,' wrote Hebborn. Although he spent a night in Blunt's bed, nothing happened due to what Hebborn referred to as their mutual 'brewer's droop'.

By his own account Hebborn produced more than a thousand drawings, allegedly by artists such as Rubens, Bruegel, Van Dyck, Poussin and Tiepolo, which were sold through respected auction houses into numerous prestigious collections. His counterfeit masterpieces were bought by the British Museum, the Metropolitan Museum of Art in New York and the National Gallery in Washington. Amusingly, he once claimed that an ink etching of Roman ruins that had hung in the Copenhagen National Gallery was his, while the gallery insisted that it was by Piranesi. His downfall came in 1978 after a London dealer realised that he had forged drawings by two different artists on the same type of paper.

Hebborn used antique brushes and reproduced old inks, but his best trick was to draw his fakes on authentic period paper from the end pages of antique print books. He prepared the paper by soaking it in infusions of tea and coffee, or by smoking it over a fire. Another ingenious scam involved painting a fake over a fake. Once the top fake was revealed by X-ray, the buyer was more likely to believe that the bottom fake was an exciting, real find.

Having the tools of the trade was one thing, but Hebborn was also an enormously talented draughtsman who would live and breathe the life of the artist he was copying at the time. 'Sometimes his paintings were more beautiful than the originals,' Colonel Roberto Conforti, head of Italy's artistic heritage squad, told the press.

What drove Hebborn to fakery when he was clearly talented in his own right? Ben Gooder, a friend and film director who made an *Omnibus* programme on Hebborn for the BBC, told me it was a revenge of sorts: 'From his childhood he was betrayed at key stages in his life by authority figures. It was revenge on a society or class that found his manners and looks rough and had excluded him. He delighted in pricking their egos and got pleasure knowing he was bettering himself.' For his part Hebborn wrote: 'The more competent the expert the more pleasure I derive from being able to lead him astray.'

However, says Gooder, 'Ultimately it became very unsatisfactory for him because the art dealers, who were selling on Hebborn's work at a grossly inflated price, were still profiting from the fakes.' He gave up faking on the publication of *Drawn to Trouble* in 1991. His exposé caused ripples of discontent in the art world and there was talk of his arrest. Four years later he published *The Art Forger's Handbook*[2] (in Italian), revealing the 'cookbook' secrets of his trade and upsetting plenty of buyers who in the past had made investments in his art in good faith. Around this time he voiced concerns that he felt threatened by those who had bought his work.

In January 1996 Hebborn received a mysterious head injury as he wandered home in Trastevere after a night's drinking. He was found by a flower pot outside his apartment door in Piazza San Giovanni del Malva, his wallet and credit cards still in his pocket. He died in hospital a few days later, as the press speculated whether he had fallen and hit his head or been bludgeoned from behind.

Janice Viarnaud, a friend of Hebborn, told me, 'He was drinking a lot and had very fragile blood vessels; a few months earlier he had knocked himself against a glass table and bled profusely.' According to Viarnaud, on the night of his death his flat was ransacked by a group of 'friends' who had keys at the time and scoured the apartment for a will. At this point he was still in hospital, not even dead. An English woman even took what she claimed to be her pots and pans back while others stole paintings.

A line was peddled to the press that the homosexual artist had been out looking for young men, but apparently he had been drinking close to his apartment with a gallery owner. The case is now officially closed by the Italian police with a verdict of accidental death, but suspicions linger.

In death there was no grand tomb topped by a copy of an ancient sculpture and sited among the other artists of Rome's Protestant Cemetery. Instead, Hebborn's ashes rest high above the plains of Lazio, in a slot in Anticoli Corrado's wall for the dead. The whole village turned out to bow their heads in respect for this extraordinary *straniero*. I wish now that I'd shared a carafe of local wine with him that afternoon in Anticoli. Then perhaps he would have taken me down through the trees to his idyllic studio and shown me some Old Masters and his recipes for deceit.

To brush up on the history of forgery visit Rome's newly refurbished Museum of Criminology,[3] which is set in a nineteenth-century prison and has a fascinating display of fakes and forgeries.

If you have enough time and patience, the odd antique bargain can be found in one of Rome's several markets, including the print market in Piazza Fontanella Borghese (near the criminology museum) and at the Porta Portese flea market in Trastevere (see the 'Designer Shops and Flea Markets' chapter, page 93). Alternatively, visit the many art and antiques galleries along the picturesque streets of Via Giulia, Via del Babuino, Via Margutta and Via del Coronari (which holds antique fairs in May and October). Cheaper deals can be found in the numerous antique-restoration shops that line Via del Pellegrino, just off Campo de' Fiori.

Finally, for a daytrip to Anticoli Corrado, take a blue COTRAL bus from Ponte Mammolo – there are two a day, in the early morning and mid-afternoon. The village has its own modern art gallery[4] with a few pictures by Hebborn and many by other local artists. The altar of the nearby church of Santa Vittoria is decorated with a painting of Christ donated by Hebborn. Over lunch at the Taverna dei Sette Peccati (Seven Sins Inn), myths about the rogue artist are served up with local specialities.

1   *Drawn to Trouble: Confessions of a Master Forger* by Eric Hebborn, Mainstream Publishing, 1991.
2   *The Art Forger's Handbook* by Eric Hebborn, Cassell Illustrated, 1997 (posthumous; an Italian edition was first published in 1995).
3   MUSEO DI CRIMINOLOGIA, 29 Via del Gonfalone, 06 688 9942, 9am–1pm & 2.30pm–6.30pm Tues & Thurs, 9am–1pm Weds, Fri & Sat, €2.
4   MUSEO D'ARTE MODERNA, 1 Piazza Santa Vittoria, Anticoli Corrado, 07 7493 6318, open 9am–1pm and 4pm–7pm daily. For tourist information for the village, 07 7493 6318.

ROME'S
RENAISSANCE
GARDENS

Unlocking green secrets

Rome is not renowned as one of Europe's most verdant capitals, and yet wherever you are in the city, if you look up and around you hints of gardens abound, from the lonesome oak tree in the corner of Piazza dello Quercia to the Amazonian palms of Piazza del Risorgimento. An ivy trellis hangs from a façade, bougainvillaea and fig trees conspicuously spill over walls, colourful geraniums fill window boxes and roof terraces are crowned with palms, cypresses and cacti. Tufts of wild rocket are even known to sprout up between the roof tiles.

I'm not sure that gardening will ever be the new rock'n'roll in Italy, a country that has always preferred its public piazzas to its private patios, but Rome is home to some splendid Renaissance gardens that were as artfully conceived as the historic buildings they abut.

As the effects of the Renaissance's building boom in Florence and Venice trickled south to Rome, the pope and aristocratic families began aping the ancient Roman patricians by constructing well-appointed villas with formal gardens. The architects wanted to pull down the high walls of medieval gardens and suffuse the plot with new meaning. For them the garden represented the first step into a fantastical world, one that formed a bridge between the wild countryside and their majestic new villas. Inspired by *The Dream of Poliphilus*, a guidebook to Renaissance gardens published in 1499, the modern idea of a garden began to take root.

The dawn of the sixteenth century also ushered in an age in which the garden became a showcase for wealth and a symbol of power. 'A Renaissance garden was never just plants,' I am told by Alessandra Vinciguerra, a garden historian and superintendent of the gardens at the American Academy in Rome[1] (its gardens are open to visits by appointment only). 'When visitors arrived at the villa of a baronial family they would have seen right away how the garden was designed. They would have read the messages it conveyed about nature and art and, most importantly, about the family.'

It was only natural that gardening, with its blend of artifice and science, would make some groundbreaking shifts during the Renaissance, a period characterised by man pitting his wits against the arbitrary forces of nature. Surrounded as cities then were by wild woods, Vinciguerra says:

> The garden became the place where man could tame nature . . . Learning how to read a garden helped the onlooker to interpret and understand nature and culture. It was common to find a statue of Pegasus, the winged horse, at the edge of a Renaissance garden, because he symbolised freedom and wilderness. Closer to the house you would find statues of Apollo and biblical figures – symbols of culture and history, the dominion of man.

This formal order was reflected in the gardens' august walkways and terraces, and stark geometrical patterns. A labyrinthal style became typical of the period, stirring both the mind and the senses. A good example is the secret gardens that flank the Galleria Borghese[2] museum which, when viewed from the loggia above as they were intended to be seen, have the appearance of an intricately patterned carpet.

The neat museum gardens contrast with the wider reaches of the public Villa Borghese park which is now studded with decapitated statues and busts missing their noble Roman noses. Once upon a time the city council kept a large stock of marble noses to replace the missing ones, but they have long since given up.

Immune to such vandalism is the nearby Villa Medici, now home to the French Academy.[3] Just north of the Spanish Steps the Villa commands a fine view over Rome. The writer H V Morton stood at its iron gate and imagined a cardinal treading the pathways in conversation with Velázquez, who stayed at the villa and painted this garden. Writing in 1873, Henry James considered the villa to be 'perhaps the most enchanting place in Rome. The part of the garden called the Boschetto has an incredible, impossible charm.' Today the Villa Medici garden has been restored to original plans and is open by appointment only. Its sixteenth-century harmony is still evident with its low, sinuous hedgerows, long gravel walkways and cypress trees.

Going from one vantage point to another, from the giddy heights of the top of St Peter's the Vatican Gardens[4] below are a healthy splash of green surrounded by the 44 hectares (109 acres) of holy turf, and beyond the Vatican's walls by compact, tawny-roofed residential districts.

As a result of 80km (50 miles) of irrigation pipes laid down by Pius XI, the lawns stay fresh and green throughout Rome's scalding summers. Previous popes have kept eagles, deer and ostriches here. Today there is just the odd gang of cats that have scaled the heights of the Vatican's walls and prowl such follies as the series of archways of clipped ilex framing the cupola of St Peter's. The gardens have one or two fountains that randomly soak visitors – arguably proof of a sense of humour within the Vatican? There's also an elegant summerhouse, or *casina*, built by Pirro Ligorio, who laid out the gardens of the Villa d'Este for Cardinal d'Este. The summerhouse is made from stone carted uphill from Domitian's stadium, which lay beneath what is now Piazza Navona, and was a favourite idyll of the ever-spiritually inclined H V Morton.

It is soothing to think of popes treading these leafy paths in solitary contemplation. Pius XII had a transparent cover built along one wall so that he could take his afternoon perambulation in all weathers. Oscar Wilde, however, in a letter to Robert Ross in 1900, was not so impressed:

> Today, on coming out of the Vatican Gallery, Greek gods and the Roman middle-classes in my brain, all marble to make the contrast worse, I found that the Vatican Gardens were open to the Bohemian and the Portuguese pilgrims. I at once spoke both languages fluently, explaining that my English dress was a form of penance, and entered the waste, desolate park, with its faded Louis XIV gardens, its sombre avenues, its sad woodland. The peacocks screamed, and I understood why tragedy dogged the gilt feet of each pontiff. But I wandered in exquisite melancholy for an hour.

Inside the gardens it is worth looking out for a series of old steps that lead to the Corridoio di Castello. This is the secret passageway that links the Vatican with Castel Sant'Angelo and through which Pope Clement VII scurried to safety during the Barbarians' vicious ransacking of Rome in 1527.

In 1505, 22 years before the Barbarians' arrival, Baldassare Peruzzi built a pretty villa on the banks of the Tiber for the rich banker Agostino Chigi. Later known as Villa Farnesina,[5] after the Farnese family ousted a bankrupt Chigi in 1577, Peruzzi built it in a way that made the gardens the main focus. An open ground-floor loggia in the wings of the villa allowed guests to look out on to the greenery and woods beyond. Raphael – who in 1518 designed splendid gardens at Villa Madama, between the Pantheon and Piazza Navona – created a kind of interior allotment by having his assistants decorate the ceiling of the loggia with pictures of flowers and vegetables. Keep your eyes peeled for the phallic cucumber fertilising a fig above the hand of Mercury. Upstairs in the Salone delle Prospettive (literally, 'Lounge of Perspectives'), where the windows had a more restricted view, trompe l'oeil frescoes create the illusion of looking out on to the contemporary Roman campagna. (Donato Bramante achieved a similar effect in the Vatican Gardens by drawing attention from the terraces and staircases out to the countryside.)

At a dead-end just across the road from Villa Farnesina are the lush and exotic Botanical Gardens (Orto Botanico).[6] Among the gardens' twenty or so sections are bamboos, ferns, plants that look like giant sea creatures, and a fascinating allotment of medicinal herbs. Their sprawling diversity is the antithesis of the meticulously trimmed Renaissance garden with all its social and philosophical compost. This is also one of Rome's most tranquil getaways when you feel you've had enough of the crowds and noisy traffic.

The magnificent evergreen magnolia opposite the entrance to the gardens is a taste of things to come – it is about 200 years old and is believed to be the first tree of its kind in Rome. The proliferation of greenery must be both a pleasing and frustrating outlook for inmates of the nearby Regina Coeli prison, many of whom in recent years have been establishment figures sentenced for white-collar crimes during the Tangentopoli investigations. They were probably just the sort of men partial to a spot of weekend gardening.

The free can climb high to the gardens' upper woodland, the last remnant of the forest once covering Rome. A graffitied pagoda is an ideal lovers' respite from which openings through ancient trees frame a view of stony Rome below. Here the peace is interrupted only by the rush of water from the mighty Acqua Paola fountain that flanks the hill, and at midday by the dull, thunderous sound of a cannon fired in commemoration of Garibaldi's victory over the papal forces in 1870. His statue rides a horse high above the gardens. For a while I thought that the Botanical Gardens, which lie directly beneath Garibaldi's cannon, were probably the least safe place to be when it is fired, but it turns out that the cannon's boom is bigger than its strike, as it fires blanks.

The monumental Baroque staircase is overgrown with plant stubble and the Tritons of the fountain appear to be afflicted with a corrosive disorder – one dreads to think what sort of message such a place would have conveyed should the Renaissance Farnese have been coming round for tea. But there is something satisfying about the natural decay of things here. It is a truly soothing place to visit first thing in the morning, or after a hearty lunch to wander its gently hilly paths through the trees.

1   AMERICAN ACADEMY IN ROME, 5 Via Angelo Masina, 06 58 461, www.aarome.org. The gardens can be visited by appointment only; visitors require a photo ID.

2   GALLERIA BORGHESE, 5 Piazzale Scipione Borghese, 06 8207 7304. The secret gardens of Villa Borghese can be visited by guided tour, 10.30am Sat, free.

3   ACADEMIE DE FRANCE A ROME, 1a Viale Trinità dei Monti, 06 6992 1653, www.villamedici.it. Visits by appointment only.

4   VATICAN GARDENS, 06 6988 4466/4587. Guided tours at 10am Tues & Thurs to Sat, Sat only in high season, €9, book one week in advance.

5   VILLA FARNESINA, 230 Via della Lungara, 06 6802 7268, open 9am–1pm daily except Sun, €4.50.

6   ORTO BOTANICO, 24 Largo Cristina di Svezia, 06 4991 7106, open 9am–6.30pm Tues to Sat, €2.06.

ANCIENT AQUEDUCTS

Picnic by the ruins

If the beauty of arriving in Rome from Fiumicino airport is the view of the Palazzo della Civiltà del Lavoro (the 'Square Colosseum', see page 83) as you approach the city's out-lying EUR district, then the bonus of travelling from Ciampino airport is the glimpses of partial aqueducts amid the countryside. Both are classically arched structures from different ages and both offer a taster of what the city holds.

Two centuries before EasyJet and Ikea invaded the Roman *campagna* the French artist Claude Lorrain captured its haunting, romantic beauty. In his paintings the ruins of Roman aqueducts stretch across the canvas like trains and the countryside is infused with a lustre exceptional to Rome. It is not exactly what you would experience today.

Now, the intermittent remains of the aqueducts are juxtaposed with the spoils of modern suburban Rome. But, for those who seek it, something of the spirit of Lorrain's paintings remains, especially when the leftover hulks of the aqueducts are seen for the first time. It's a feeling akin to the thrill of spotting a wild animal on safari.

In fact, there is something almost prehistoric about these discreet ruins. The writer Henry James described them in his collection *Italian Hours* (1909) as a 'long gaunt file of arches . . . their jagged ridge stretching away like the vertebral column of some monstrous mouldering skeleton.'

Fortunately one of the most evocative sections still standing is accessible by public transport (metro station Giulio Agricola on the A line). The combination of antique ruins and nature makes the Parco degli Acquedotti a memorable place for a walk and a picnic. From the station head for the carbuncle of a modern church – a rare sight in Rome – on Via Lemonia; cross over Spartacus Avenue (all the streets and metro stations in this residential area are named after famous Romans) and pick up a tray of sliced pizza or some goodies from the PAM supermarket.

Pass through the first line of arches to a grassy ledge where it feels like you are on the very edge of the city. This is as close as it gets to Claude's terrain, minus the train to Naples rattling between the converging stilts of the aqueducts. Here among the joggers, stray cats, poppies and alfalfa you can pick wild rocket as a topping for your takeaway pizza and, depending on the time of year, plummy grapes from the overspill of the row of allotments. Ask the pottering gardeners nicely and you may be given some peaches or figs for your picnic. Beyond the allotments it becomes jungle-like and a dump for stolen scooters and junkies' syringes.

The park, also known as Parco Lemonia, is criss-crossed by the substantial remains of four aqueducts: Anio Vetus, Acqua Marcia (also bearing Acqua Tepula and Acqua Giulia), Acqua Claudia (also bearing Anio Novus), and the Acqua Felice conduit built by Pope Sixtus V in 1585. Classical Rome had eleven ancient aqueducts; the longest, Anio Novus, was 95km (59 miles) long; the first, the Appia, was built in 312 BC, and the last, the Alexandrina, in AD 226.

But the arches that graced the countryside were just the tip of the iceberg, as four-fifths of Rome's 500km (300-mile) water network was constructed underground in channels bored through the rock. The conduits were often raised on arches as they approached the city to give the water added momentum, or to carry it across valleys and plains. Today, the longest series of arches above ground is about 10km (6 miles) long. The constant flow relied on gravity not pumps, and filled cisterns, bathhouses, gardens and public fountains. The water system served a city of one million people, providing more than one cubic metre of water per day for each inhabitant – the sort of quota that today's Sicilians would betray their mothers for during the regular summer droughts.

Writing in the first century in his *Naturalis Historia*, Pliny the Elder considered the aqueduct to be the most marvellous engineering feat in the world. In fact, it was advanced systems like this that distinguished the Romans from the Greeks as great practical engineers and the true forerunners of our sanitised modern way of life. A system that brought fresh supplies of man's most precious commodity right into the city was indeed a remarkable achievement.

That the aqueducts survived at all is quite a feat. In the sixth century AD the Goths besieged Rome and severed almost all the aqueducts leading into the city. The only one that continued to flow was Acqua Virgo, which ran entirely underground. Repairs by a succession of emperors, conquerors and popes revived a few of the aqueducts during the Middle Ages. But most of the population had to resort to the Tiber as the only source of water – it is for this reason that the medieval buildings of Rome lie almost exclusively in the two great bends of the river, the Campo Marzio and

Trastevere. It was not until the Renaissance that the Eternal City was once again provided with flowing aqueducts and lavish fountains.

In broad terms most of the aqueducts brought cool, clear water from the springs to the east of the city. In the eighteenth century, during the great heat of summer, the conduits carrying away the fountain water were closed and the fountains were allowed to overflow and fill Piazza Navona – built above the ancient stadium of the emperor Domitian – knee-deep in water. (Just north of the piazza at 16 Piazza di Tor Sanguigna you can still see some remains of the original arena, sunk below street level; for guided tours on weekend mornings call 06 6710 3819.)

Just as there is an abundant choice of mineral waters available today – the preferred Roman choice seems to be the fizzy, sodium-rich Ferrarelle – the waters of each aqueduct had their own characteristics. Acqua Giulia was slightly sparkling; Acqua Tepula, as its name suggests, was always tepid; and Acqua Marcia was known for its health-giving qualities. The Acqua Virgo completed in 19 BC has been providing water ever since – it supplies the area around the Spanish Steps and the Trevi Fountain and is said to make the best coffee, the ultimate litmus test, in Rome. Even today some of the older kitchens in central Rome have a special tap emitting Acqua Paola water which is used for washing up.

In spite of a suspected terrorist plot to poison Rome's water supply in February 2002 – police seized 4kg of a cyanide compound in a bag and a map highlighting the city's water pipelines and showing the entrances to the US embassy on Via Veneto – the never-ending flow of fresh water is one of the treats of the Eternal City. Many other Mediterranean cities lack this simple luxury, and Londoners would be desperate if they had to rely on their mainly defunct public drinking fountains.

When in Rome make sure you taste the waters from one of the two thousand *nasoni* (big nose) fountains located throughout the city. The street tap takes its name from the curved pipe, resembling an emperor's proboscis, that protrudes from the cistern. By plugging the end of the pipe with your finger the water spurts out from a small hole on the bridge of the pipe – ideal for accidentally spraying an 'enemy'. As you quench your thirst think of the water's source; much of it still journeys from natural springs.

CULTURAL ROME

ROMAN GRAFFITI

The art of vandalism

Rome deserves its tag as the world's greatest outdoor museum. As well as its exquisite ruins the Eternal City has a distinguished tradition of public art, from ancient Roman sculpture and early Christian mosaics to the Renaissance and Baroque masterpieces of Bramante, Michelangelo and Bernini. Recently, however, many of its historic buildings and monuments have been besmirched by clearly less talented 'artists'. They have monikers such as Dumbo, Gucci, Headache and Blast and, unlike the Vandals who ransacked Rome in the fifth century, express themselves with aerosols.

Whereas in other capitals graffiti is largely confined to railway tunnels and grisly suburbs, central Rome is awash with it like an insidious skin disease, spreading across statues, fountains and its colourful façades while the city slumbers.

Declarations of undying love, coarse football rivalries, and political symbols and slogans, the most frequent of late being: 'Neither Bush nor Islam', provide common external decoration. Young Romans seem to be as opinionated as their elders are garrulous. Much of the writing, however, is just the squiggled signatures of what Italians call 'the writers', and is as indecipherable, at least to most locals, as Arabic script.

Fine examples of true graffiti (inscriptions or drawings carved on to a surface) can be seen on the façade of the sixteenth-century Palazzo Ricci on Via di Monserrato near Piazza Farnese. Examples of the reinvented modern craft are everywhere, but particularly rife on the Colle Oppio hill above the Colosseum, along the banks of the Tiber, in Testaccio and San Lorenzo, on the Liberty villas of Borgo Trento, around the stadium and on trains to Ostia.

Worryingly for the mayor, Walter Veltroni, tourists – Rome's life blood – have started to notice the city's decline in mural standards. Visitors from the much-cleaned-up east coast cities of America and other spruced up European capitals are flabbergasted to find a building in which Raphael had a hand defaced by kids.

'It's like one of the most beautiful cities in the world just got tattooed, badly,' says an American tour guide. 'Spoiling a ghetto is one thing, but scrawling on precious works of art is sacrilegious.'

Things aren't much better underground. So completely smothered is Rome's fleet of underground trains that it's impossible for passengers to see at which station they're arriving. On a website featuring graffiti in Rome one man claims to have daubed an entire train on the A-line and another to have been chased into a tunnel and shot at by frustrated station guards.

Of course, graffiti is not a new blight for Rome – a carved sign has been found from Caesar's time begging citizens not to scribble on private property – but the situation has never been so messy.

A few limp-wristed preventive measures from the mayor's office in response to the mushrooming problem have not been very successful. 'No graffiti' signs bearing a black spray-can crossed through with a red line and a warning of fines were erected throughout the city at historic sites, but the signs themselves were defaced – proof that mere signage, like traffic lights and parking zones, is not enough to make Italians toe the line.

Likewise, during frequent protest marches when monuments and statues along the route are covered up to protect them from graffiti, the protesters just aim their *bombolette*, or spray-cans, elsewhere. 'We can't wrap up the entire city,' says Sabato Carbone of the city's poetically named Office of Urban Decorum. 'If they want to make a statement on a historic building then Rome has no shortage of targets.'

Part of the protesters' route, Via dei Fori Imperiali, which runs through the ancient forums to the Colosseum, is one of the worst-hit areas. The walls are covered with multicoloured scrawl like the over-doodled pages of a bored student's notebook. What can be read attacks globalisation and Berlusconi's government, and expresses racial intolerance towards black people and Jews. The Celtic cross, hammer and sickle and the wolf's head of Roma football club are recurrent symbols. Ironically the road is an act of vandalism itself, brutally carved up by Mussolini in the 1930s to serve as a victory parade path.

'It's becoming worse,' says Maurizio Venafro, head of All Clean Rome, the government-backed graffiti removal team. 'It's a battle of wills and it's difficult to stop them as they go to extreme measures by working at night. Often we will clean a wall and then the next morning it's covered again. It's like an ironic game for them: the more historic the place, the greater the transgression.'

A popular canvas, according to Venafro, because it is a symbol of the state, is the Vittorio Emanuele II monument in Piazza Venezia. The mammoth, dazzling white edifice is also guarded by soldiers which increases the risk factor and thereby the thrill and kudos for the graffitists.

In an effort to stay a step ahead of the writers, All Clean has introduced round-the-clock security and now coats walls with a special transparent film to prevent new graffiti from lasting. This wax-based coating has been applied to most of Rome's trains. 'Eventually the graffiti gangs will go elsewhere,' says Venafro hopefully.

In the meantime, with stop-gap measures failing and removal costs exceeding €50,000 a month, the city has decided to crack down on graffiti artists. The Office of Urban Decorum has launched a new task force of 150 officers with the power to fine those caught in the act, and fines have been hiked from €120 to anything up to €3,000. The new crop of bylaws also includes a fine for residents hanging washing out of their windows, a traditionally picturesque feature of the city's oldest streets.

Romans, many of whom seem to accept graffiti as if it were outdoor wallpaper, expect little to change. When a similar scheme was tried in Milan in 2002, only one graffitist was apprehended. Graffiti has in fact become so much a part of Roman visual culture that the tangled words that recently covered orange buses were not the work of teenage crews armed with aerosols, but part of a smart advertising campaign for the latest Isabel Allende book. In a drive to stop kids daubing public walls, the film studios at Cinecittà have provided a series of giant metal walls for special, authorised murals by graffiti artists. 'We believe that graffiti can be considered as an expression of juvenile creativity, particularly when it is done without bringing offence or vandalism,' says Luca Odevaine of the city council.

Encouragingly, public art of a different sort has already helped to reduce graffiti. At the nineteen metro stations that have been revamped with mosaics by contemporary artists such as Joe Tilson (at Ottaviano) and Piero D'Orazio (at Colosseo), the return of graffiti has been noticeably absent.

However, when faith in the authorities fails in Rome, you can always invoke God's protection – this is after all a holy city. At the end of a Sunday morning service at the American Episcopal church of St Paul's Within the Walls, the congregation is led out on to Via Nazionale by the Reverend Michael Vono. Following a blessing for the freshly restored façade and its mosaics by George William Breck, for many years the Director of the American Academy in Rome, he adds: 'And please, please Lord, we pray that no one writes on this wall. Amen.'

❝ Try telling the Reverend Reginald Foster that Latin is a dead language. You would receive an impassioned rant from this ruddy-faced Carmelite monk who has dedicated a large chapter of his recent life to keeping the forerunner of English and Romance languages alive. He does so by teaching students at Rome's prestigious Catholic Gregorian University, and a diehard group of Latinists at a summer school he runs in Rome each year for free. 'To learn Latin you don't have to be particularly intelligent,' he professes. 'But you do have to have character.'

In his official function Foster translates documents for Pope John Paul II. He has a spartan office in the Vatican's Apostolic palace just a few Raphael frescoes away from the Pope's own bureau. For fifty years or so (he's in his sixties) Latin has been part of his regimen and he remembers the days when masses were still conducted in Latin, before the second Vatican council heralded the decline and fall of his beloved language in the 1960s.

Reggie, as his students know him, is peerless among teachers of Latin. In his lessons students are inspired to bask in the glory of a forgotten language. 'For me Latin is glorious,' he says. 'Like Bach, Handel and Bernini.'

He knows how to promote the primary Latin texts – the letters from such perceptive writers as Seneca, Pliny the Elder and his favourite, Cicero – and how to revive flagging interest with gossipy tales about the authors. Rather than separating himself from today's blink-and-it's-gone world and its rapid, abbreviated forms of communication, Foster's profound knowledge and his ability to share it with other generations keep him in touch with the world. As a colleague of his once said, he is able to give you an appreciation of something much bigger than yourself.

But above all Father Foster is serious about leading the battle to keep from extinction a 'dinosaur' of languages, once spoken by all Romans – emperors, philosophers, centurions and slaves. Outside of the classroom he has made sure that Latin is an option on the cash machines of the Vatican City bank: 'Inserito scidulum quaeso faciundam ut cognoscas rationem' or 'please insert the small card in order to proceed'. If you are lucky enough to take a stroll around the city in his company, you will find that he relishes translating Latin inscriptions on church façades and ruins – an enviable skill to possess in Rome.

Latin lovers with advanced language skills can find out more about his summer school at www.latin.org/latin/foster/FAQ.html, or by writing to Reginald Foster OCD at Teresianum, 5a Piazza San Pancrazio, 00152 Rome. The course is free but donations are accepted towards the running costs.

Alternatively, free Latin classes for English- and French-speaking tourists are offered by Rome's regional government, along with two historical societies. The courses feature basic history and language lessons and use a comic book starring 'Caesar' – e-mail ilregnodicamelot@libero.it for details.

GLADIATOR
SCHOOL

Battling with swords and sandals

'Either I kill my father, or he kills me, at least once a week,' says Morpheus, an amiable Roman who, along with his parents, plays a central role at Rome's gladiator school, the Scuola Gladiatori Roma,[1] where I am going to train à la Spartacus. The school is part of the Gruppo Storico Romano, a cultural association founded in 1994 which recreates the lifestyles of Romans living in Nero's time.

As modern Romans poured home from work in their cars, 23-year-old Morpheus (whose real name is Guido Pecorelli) came out to meet me at the start of the Via Appia Antica wearing a worsted tunic with a leather pouch, sandals strapped around his calves, a protective leather cover on one forearm and wielding a short, weighty *glado*, or sword.

I had gone halfway down the gravelly country road that leads to the school when I had to perform a most unancient Roman act: call Morpheus on his mobile phone, as two fierce dogs were blocking my path. Perhaps this was the gods sending me my first test, like Aeneas having to overcome Cerberus to enter the underworld. Morpheus fearlessly sent them packing with a hard stare and a swoosh of his sword. I knew that once I had completed my training I wouldn't be expected to fight wild animals, but this wasn't a great start.

The gladiator school is in a small Roman fort made from pencil-shaped pieces of tree trunk. It is decked with vines and plaster-cast busts and has signs carved in Latin indicating the training ground, the taverna, the arena and the stage. Behind the school trains rattle past headed to Naples and buses come and go from their depot. Busying themselves around the fort are Romans dressed in togas, short tunics and various gladiatorial outfits. It feels like I'm on the set of one of those TV history experiments.

The training area is a small hall clad like a museum of ancient weapons and armour, all painstakingly made by members of the group. There's a row of helmets with meshed face guards, all shapes and sizes of swords, daggers, spears and shields, arm and shin guards and tinny armadillo-like armour.

Swinging a large hammer above his head is a hulky man called Orseus, dressed only in a short, pleated 'skirt' and who looks as though he could probably use a breastplate. He is engaged in combat with an equally robust female gladiator, dressed in an imperial white tunic with red trim and armed with a sword. In Ancient Roman times women gladiators were called *provocatrix*. They wore a girdle that left one breast exposed and would usually fight either other women or dwarves. After a series of swings, thrusts and groans our *provocatrix* (breast unexposed) ends up, rather ungracefully, prostrate with Orseus's laced leather boot poised just above her throat ready to bring his hammer down on to her skull. This is pretend stuff, but still the hairs go up on the back of my neck.

I change into a white cotton tunic tied by a leather belt and Morpheus hands me what looks like a toy cricket bat. He guides me through the six basic movements of attack: split crown of head in two; chop off head at neck, forehand and backhand; slice off lower leg, forehand and backhand, and run through the belly. At the school they instruct you to bring the weapon within an inch of your opponent's body. Wooden sword or not, this gives you a taste of the mortal terror that the defeated must have endured briefly.

'It's about strategy as much as strength,' says Morpheus. I feel encouraged. 'If you shatter the knee of the big guy he will come tumbling down.'

Along with the physical strategy there seems so much to learn about gladiators. A prize fighter would have had Olympic hero status, complete with a rigid training routine, a coach, an agent, a patron and groupies. Many of the accoutrements were made to handicap the fighters in order to prolong the contest. 'Like boxing today,' says Morpheus, 'no one wanted to pay to see a knockout in the first round.'

Given that visibility is almost zero through most of the helmets' visors, I can't help thinking that this is the sort of handicap that could drastically shorten encounters, too. My own vision is further limited when, after an hour or so and I'm starting to get the hang of it, I clash heads with my beefy opponent and my glasses snap like matchsticks and fall to the ground. I feel like the square schoolboy in a playground bundle, but between us we tape up the glasses and press on.

Adding a shield to the equation demands deft co-ordination. The net, too, is tricky. It takes me twenty flings, tracing an arc to and fro, to hook an immobile chair; trying to hook the crest on the top of a nimble opponent's helmet requires years of practice. Fearing that I could do myself and others an injury, I leave the trident and mace to the pros. The trainee gladiators occasionally suffer broken bones in their hands and scratched or swollen thumbs, but the weapons, although heavy, are blunt.

Most of the group are typically well-fed, rasping-voiced Romans, and mostly ancient history buffs in ordinary jobs – bankers, builders, cleaners and students – who come for the culture and camaraderie. They each assume an ancient Roman character as soon as they step out of their suits and switch off their mobile phones; Morpheus is a Briton captured and brought to Rome to work in the court of Nerone (the group president, Sergio Iacomoni).

The role-playing acts as both therapy and exercise. 'Here we get away from our jobs and relax. The Romans knew how to live an honest life without too many rules,' says Iacomoni. Morpheus, who has shed an amazing 25kg since he began training two years ago, says 'Fighting with a sword and shield for seven minutes is like a workout at the gym. Eastern arts like karate don't give me the same sense of spiritual connection as gladiator fighting. After all, I am Roman and these are my roots.'

The group already stages historical shows – they have fought in the Ancient Roman theatre at Ostia Antica and in the gladiators' gym at Pompeii, and hold annual parades through the Roman Forum and the Circus Maximus – and many of the members hope one day to fight in the Colosseum. An ambition that could possibly be realised now the city council is once again allowing performances to be staged there. In the meantime, before a candlelit feast in honour of Jove, the gladiators put on a spectacle. When they emerge from a tunnel of dry ice to chants of their fighting name and a drum beat, it feels like watching TV, and sure enough in the background I discern the soundtrack from Ridley Scott's *Gladiator*.

A lanky American who has been training with the group for two months tells me that Orseus (the bear-like one) told him he wants to know what it's like to kill. Orseus is a giant, almost double my size, and ours would be the sort of freakish David-and-Goliath match that the Roman crowd would have gone wild for, but fortunately I am not billed against Orseus. When he does fight, the head of his long mallet flies off into the crowd. Luckily no one is hurt.

Instead, I put up a brave, quite defensive fight against Morpheus that lasts an admirable four minutes, though I feel vulnerable in my taped-up glasses. Then, like a fire flare, my trusty *magister* (teacher) brings an axe head within inches of my face. I can smell the metal. A cold feeling washes over me, but after what seems like an age, Morpheus smiles. He's used to this killing lark.

As I walked back late at night along the Via Appia Antica, over its mossy flagstones and past the catacombs towards the civilised centre of the Eternal City, I imagined hearing the cries of the crucified gladiators lining the Appian Way, or Regina Viarum ('Queen of Roads'), all the way to Magna Grecia, the Greek-occupied southern tip of ancient Italy. I straightened my glasses and quickened my step.

1   SCUOLA GLADIATORI ROMA, 18 Via Appia Antica, 06 5160 7951, www.gsr-roma.com. A two-month course consisting of two lessons a week costs €112.

❝ Without the help of any signage I knew that I was at the Colosseum metro stop. It wasn't just the modern bathroom-style mosaics that I'd read about as part of a project to spruce up Rome's underground. Rather, propping up the station's

snack booth were three centurions smoking and
sipping espresso.

They were taking a break from their duty across
the road where they charge tourists a sometimes hefty
fee to be photographed with them outside Rome's
best known landmark. But in 2003 Rome's council
gave a big thumbs-down to this increasing band of
freelancers in ancient garb of variable authenticity.
What the spurious Spartacuses do is 'ugly' said the
council which is keen to do away with the sort of
shuckster behaviour that gives Rome a bad name.

Now would-be Caesars and Caligulas have to buy a
licence to prove they have a clean criminal record,
and adhere to asking for a single fee to be snapped (€5
instead of the €20 that was not an uncommon
request). They have also been required to wear
authentic outfits – knee-high strappy leather sandals,
plumed helmets, gold-sprayed metal breast-plates and
embroidered tunics – though how the council's
fashion police enforce such realism is uncertain.

Roberto Cohen, head of the Roman Centurions
Association, a group of about forty costumed
centurions, gladiators and emperors who ply their
trade in the environs of the Colosseum, told me: 'We
are pleased with the rules because it affirms that we
have an official profession.'

But what are rules for in Rome if not for
circumventing? I still witnessed the odd Lazio shirt
poking out from beneath a breastplate, and jeans
showing below a tunic. And turf wars have
occasionally erupted between rival centurions vying
for the sunniest and most lucrative spot for photos.

'Do you want your wife killed?' says one gladiator in well-rehearsed English, wooden sword raised, to a passing couple. He has been on the gladiator beat for seven years and takes offence at any suggestion that his work is not a proper job – on a freezing January morning it would need a brave man to argue with him. 'Oh, what hard work it is killing all these Christians,' he says, mock stabbing a woman among a small group of nuns who scuttle away suitably horrified.

While the council is crusading to sweep away this battalion of faux centurions, perhaps its next target could be the notorious *pappagalli* (parrots), the bronzed Romeos who prey on foreign women of any age at the city's tourist sights in search of a balmy afternoon's carnal pleasure. And then, perhaps, lazy waiters, reckless drivers, tireless bureaucrats . . . but, then again, Rome wouldn't be Rome without its jocular stereotypes.

CINECITTÀ

The city of cinema

Film studios by virtue of their sheer size are often located in the most godforsaken corners of a city. The 40-hectare (99-acre) plot of Cinecittà is no exception. The Americans famously called it 'Hollywood on the Tiber', but the murky waters of the ancient river are nowhere to be seen. Instead you surface from the eponymous underground station to eight lanes of bumper-to-bumper traffic on Via Tuscolana in southeast Rome – the sort of noisy, infernal gridlock depicted in Federico Fellini's *Roma*. Here you are neither in nor out of the city's urban perimeter. Fortunately – before you clamour for ear muffs and a smog mask – you are right outside the entrance of Cinecittà.

Pronounced 'chinnay-chee-tah', Cinecittà means quite literally 'City of Cinema'. It is one of many 'cities' within Rome. To pass beneath its name mounted above the entrance in upper-case 1930s typeface is to enter into another world, a sort of Pompeii of Italian cinema – a world steeped in history and myth. Terry Gilliam, who directed *The Adventures of Baron Munchausen* at Cinecittà in 1987, called it 'that faded old terracotta bitch – seductress of the great, famous and mad.'

The studio was built by Mussolini in 1936 as a propa-ganda film factory. Some highlights from its impressive pedigree include the chariot race from *Ben-Hur* (1959), recently voted in the all-time top ten action-film stunts; Sergio Leone's spaghetti westerns; the fiery saga between Richard Burton and Elizabeth Taylor on the doomed set of *Cleopatra* (1963); and the indelible image of Anita Ekberg, all blonde tresses and cleavage, paddling through a mock Trevi Fountain in *La Dolce Vita* (1960).

Once inside it's like being on a Roman holiday camp, with its salmon stucco bungalows, umbrella pine trees and broken plaster-cast columns, among which there are scores of people cycling between its 22 stages. *Roman Holiday* starring Audrey Hepburn and Gregory Peck was actually filmed here in 1956.

One recent visitor was Martin Scorsese, who spent seven months in the Roman sunshine filming *Gangs of New York*, during which time he used a golf buggy to move around the place.

Like in the movies, the concepts of time and place shift easily here. A corner of Scorsese's 1850s New York set has already been prettified with pastel colours and shutters for an Italian film set one hundred years later in Venice. At the end of the now ghostly fake street, beyond the confines of the studios, there are ordinary apartment blocks whose film-buff residents allegedly train their binoculars on sets in the hope of catching a glimpse of the Hollywood heroes.

Weary extras, who worked 18-hour days for €80, told me that Scorsese was fiercely protective of his work in progress. He ejected one woman for taking photos and had her camera film destroyed. In the combative tradition of Burton and Taylor, the slanging matches between lead star Leonardo DiCaprio and director were supposedly wild. Tempers were not helped by reports in the Italian papers that DiCaprio looked pasty and bloated as a result of too much pasta and Roman nightlife.

Stage 5 is a 0.29 hectare (31,000 square-foot) hangar – the biggest soundstage in Europe. Fellini made all but one of his films here and mementoes of his extraordinary career are littered throughout the estate – the ten-foot gilded statue of Christ that hangs from a helicopter at the opening of *La Dolce Vita* and the colossal head of Venus from *Casanova* are just two examples. He once said, 'As long as Cinecittà exists, I feel comforted.' When Il Maestro died in 1993 thousands of Romans paid their respects at his wake held on Stage 5. Scorsese, who grew up on a diet of post-war Italian cinema and who ran operations for *Gangs of New York* from Fellini's office above Stage 5, said: 'Going through those doors every morning and being hit with the feeling that *8½* and some of the greatest films ever made were shot there, it's humbling.'

One of the attractions of Cinecittà to filmmakers is its superb record of set construction. In the space of an hour I walked down a cobblestoned nineteenth-century Broadway to a tourist-free church of St Francis of Assisi – undamaged by the earthquake that struck its original in 1997 – and on to first-century Jerusalem, where Mel Gibson was wrapping up his film *The Passion of the Christ*, the story of the Crucifixion. Incongruously, a copy of the pink sports paper *Gazzetta dello Sport* had been left behind by workmen in the Temple of King Herod.

The De Angelis family who make the props and sets have been working at Cinecittà since it opened. In the yard outside the 'Scultura' office, among the fountains from *Gladiator* (2000), the family is casting moulds with liquid fibre glass. Block by block the buildings are skilfully produced by hand, and not stamped or mass produced as in

America, an amiable Signora De Angelis, wife of the boss, tells me. Then, like pieces of Lego, the blocks are attached to a basic wooden frame, with impressive results. Although Rome can't be built in a day, within just a few months this family could build an optimum replica Eternal City. 'We are always working to impossible deadlines,' says Signora De Angelis, without a grudge. And that set, too, like all the cities they have built, real and fantasy, would be temporarily recycled then crushed by machines. 'That's just the way it is,' says De Angelis with a typically Roman shrug of acceptance.

One compensation is that she gets to meet the stars. According to De Angelis Mel Gibson has a 'holy aura of goodness' and Sylvester Stallone is 'big hearted'. She proudly tells me that she looks after Sly's dog, Milo, who couldn't fly home after *Cliffhanger* (1993) due to an ear problem.

The sculpture hall itself is a junkyard of Italian masterpieces stuffed wall-to-ceiling with statues, busts and ornaments. A cobwebbed copy of Michelangelo's *David* dwarfs his *Pietà*; the Three Graces dance around the Laocoön and a bust of Il Duce lies discarded in the corner. There are Art Nouveau lamps from Pasolini's *Salo*, the ceiling from Visconti's *Il Gattopardo*, Egyptian tombs from *Cleopatra*, swords from *Ben-Hur* and row after row of shelves housing the heads of emperors, popes and kings. If these were the genuine article this dusty collection would be the most valuable in the world. Film fans would love to get their hands on this sort of memorabilia.

And perhaps soon they will be able to indulge themselves. Cinecittà, currently closed to the public, has plans for a €200 million theme park along the lines of Universal Studios in Hollywood. It will be 'a unique theme park that will offer both fun and culture – a fantastical journey into movie magic and history,' the studios' marketing manager informs me. One idea is to recreate the chariot race from *Ben-Hur*. Now that alone would be worth the trip out on the underground.

NUOVO
SACHER
CINEMA

Satire, politics and chocolate cake

A small handwritten sticker indicates that no. 1 Largo Ascianghi is the cinema of the actor and director Nanni Moretti. The Cinema Nuovo Sacher[1] is located in Trastevere in a former building of the Fascist Dopolavoro organisation. Above the entrance an arc of colourful mosaics depicts images of music, drama, philosophy and war. These are all ingredients in Moretti's own films, the latter referring to his battle against the inertia and hypocrisy of Italians. A motto on the side of a nearby tatty former Fascist youth building: '*Necessario vincere, più necessario combattere*' ('It's necessary to win, but more important to fight') seems to inform Moretti's role as a leading figure in the anti-government *girotondo* movement.

Moretti bought the cinema as a response to the limited distribution of independent and foreign arthouse films in Rome. Acclaimed foreign films are shown here in their original language, as well as quality Italian pictures, and it hosts a short film festival in July. In the summer there is also an outdoor arena at the back.

Given that his country thrives on conformity Moretti is a bit of an oddity, though to meet him you wouldn't think so. Dressed casually in jacket and corduroys, when we meet he looks every bit the well-groomed Italian a year short of fifty. But his sartorial ease conceals a maverick director, who writes and stars in his own films – gently satiric forays into the ailing condition of mankind, Italy and himself. A gangly, pensive leftie with a neat beard he is as well known in Italy as fellow comic Roberto Benigni of *Life is Beautiful* fame. Abroad, however, where French and Latin American films flow freely but Italian films are harder to come by, Moretti remains relatively unknown.

Perhaps that's because his films aren't of the nostalgic variety deliberately prettified to export Italy's image of beauty. Think *Cinema Paradiso* or *Il Postino*. Rather, in order to calm his fears, Moretti arms himself with irony and dares to confront issues – not always head-on, but in his own idiosyncratic way. As such, discovering Moretti's films is like finding an undiscovered corner of Italy.

Arguably the leading exponent among Italy's post-'maestro' filmmakers, Moretti claims he doesn't feel 'paralysed' by the responsibility to a lineage that includes Fellini, Pasolini and Bertolucci. 'As a filmgoer I remain fond of the cinema d'auteur of the Sixties. They were films that were unsatisfied with both the cinema and society they'd inherited. So through their work they proposed a different approach to reality without losing sight of the need to make a good film.'

Moretti has always had clear ideas about how to make a meaningful film. In 1973 he was rejected by the National Film School and began making his own short Super-8 films. Since then he has maintained a certain distance from the mainstream of Italian cinema and identifies three consistent strands to his work that came 'naturally' to him: 'To be in front of the camera, as well as behind it. Not just as an actor, but also as a person. To talk about my own social, political and generational realities. And to tell all my stories with an ironic tone.' The latter is a quality much undervalued in a country that still shows Benny Hill on primetime TV.

Increasingly stimulated by politics, Moretti set out to fulfil his filmmaking criteria. His first acclaimed feature (*Ecce Bombo*, 1978) was a laconic swipe at the inertia of his own post-1968 generation. Then throughout the 1980s he played an angry, nerve-jangling alter-ego Michele, who in turn plays an Oedipal director (*Sogni d'Oro/Golden Dreams*, 1981), a psychopathic teacher (*Bianca*, 1984), a priest (*La Messa è Finita/The Mass is Over*, 1985), and a Commie water-polo player (*Palombella Rossa/The Red Polo Ball*, 1989). Michele, in whatever lead, always seems to be close to breakdown and rants against institutional corruption and personal difficulties.

By the late 1980s Moretti felt that filmmaking in Italy had grown stale and was resting on its past laurels. He sought a more innovative way of making films. The result was *Dear Diary* (1995) and *Aprile* (1998) – films which try to tell essentially political stories 'in a more personal, freer, less traditional way'.

Dear Diary was his first film to gain a release outside of Italy. In it Moretti takes the viewer on a personal odyssey. He winds through an empty Rome in August on his Vespa celebrating the striking residential villas off the tourist track in Monteverde Vecchio and Garbatella, disappears to a volcanic island in search of quiet, and battles in exasperation with an inadequate healthcare system to find a cure for his cancer. The cancer is real and to prove it he includes home-movie footage of his chemotherapy treatment. In the year of *Pulp Fiction*, Moretti's film scooped the Director's Prize at Cannes and was a taste of things to come.

Eight years later, in 2001, Moretti triumphed at Cannes with *The Son's Room*. It was the first time that an Italian had won the Palme d'Or since Ermanno Olmi in 1978. 'It was like not having won the World Cup for 92 years,' he says, counting in fours on his fingers. 'And a victory away from home is always worth more.'

It is his compulsive nature, both on and off screen, that has earned Moretti the tag of a Roman Woody Allen. It is one that he is keen to dispel. 'It's wrong because he makes one film a year and I can't keep up with that,' says Moretti, clearly enunciating each syllable. 'I'm not only a director, I have my own production company, cinema and annual festival in Rome. True, we both talk about our own worlds, but he often sets his films in other eras. I've seen all his films and I really like them, but they've not influenced mine.'

Independence is vital to Moretti. Since 1986 he has owned a production company, Sacher Films. 'It gives me the flexibility to make the type of film I want to make. That's tricky when you have a conventional relationship with the film producer.' His company gives him an autonomy second to none in a country where production is monopolised by a handful of 'popular film' producers, one of whom is the Prime Minister Silvio Berlusconi.

Moretti grimaces when I mention Berlusconi. In the past few years, Moretti has expanded his political role and become the vocal figurehead of the popular grassroots movement known as the *girotondo* (merry-go-round), in which citizens of all ages and parties join hands and circle public buildings to protest against Berlusconi's policies. Moretti is baffled, even embarrassed, by the fact that the head of democratic Italy effectively owns and controls all the state TV channels. He asks me if it could happen in

England: Tony Blair with the BBC channels in his personal portfolio. I think not.

However, Moretti's worst fears under Berlusconi's centre-right coalition are not for film directors, but for magistrates: 'Some laws have been passed that make it more difficult for the magistrates to work. The politics of the Right are not free; it's all caught up in the personal and judicial problems of Berlusconi. I fear that he will do a worse job than even Mrs Thatcher did in England.' In this mode Moretti could talk for Italy, and fortunately, through his films, he sometimes does.

1   CINEMA NUOVO SACHER, 1 Largo Ascianghi, 06 581 8116.
       Foreign films are usually shown in their original language (*VO –
       versione originale*) on Mon and Tues.

❝ It is common knowledge in Rome that the award-winning actor-director is addicted to the products of the Valzani bakery (37a/b Via del Moro, 06 580 3792, open 9am–8.30pm daily) near his cinema, which serves the best *sacher torte* in Rome – Moretti named both his cinema and production company after the Austrian chocolate speciality. In his film *Bianca*, Moretti stares longingly through the window of Valzani and is astounded that a friend has never tasted *sacher*.

True, the window display at Valzani, in business since 1925, is enough to stop you in your tracks. Rich chocolate cakes, *sacher torte* and Roman classics such as *pangiallo* (a delicious fruitcake) and *panpepato* (made with honey, chocolate and pepper) tempt even the strictest dieter. 'If you're not supposed to eat sinful sweet things then you're best to stay away,'

mamma Virginia Valzani tells me. She adds that Moretti
– who she affectionately calls a '*bravo ragazzo*' ('good
lad') – has made the chocolate cake popular again,
and he regularly dispatches a runner here for his
afternoon fix of chocolate. Valzani encourages visitors
to taste before buying, and sells shiny red gift boxes
filled with handmade sweets (priced €7 to €20).

ROMA
VS
LAZIO

Football frenzy in a city of two halves

A survey in Rome's daily *Corriere dello Sport* newspaper rates the capital's biannual league match between Roma and Lazio as the 'hottest' of all of Italy's football derbies. On the Monday morning after every Roma–Lazio Sunday clash the same broadsheet paper dedicates its first fifteen pages to the derby, covering it from every conceivable angle, as well as countless more pages during the run-up to the fixture.

No event galvanises and divides the city like the derby. In the week leading up to the encounter speculation and gesticulation in the bars and at office watercoolers is about little else. Local radio stations are jammed with frothy derby debate. There may be billions of Roman Catholics in the world, but on a derby Sunday the 80,000-strong crowd at the Olympic Stadium a mile north of the Vatican outnumbers the pilgrims who gather in St Peter's Square to see and hear the frail and distant figure of Pope John Paul II.

A love–hate rivalry exists between fans of the two teams, their relationship being what the papers describe as a 'volatile cousinship'. Each team has assumed its own Roman identity. Traditionally, Roma fans (*Romanisti*) consider themselves to be urbane and liberal, the true descendants of the city's mighty heritage, with blanket support in the former working-class districts of Testaccio and Garbatella, while their archrivals consider them to be dishonest and lowly braggarts. The Lazio fans (*Laziali*) are supposed to be the wealthy self-made folk from Prati, Parioli and the outlying Castelli hills with a reputation for links to the far Right – or, according to Roma fans, they are knuckle-dragging bumpkins, *burrini* in local dialect. These stereotypes may reflect a broader historical fan base and be the source of much pointscoring between the two, but today fans of both teams can be found in all areas of the city.

When a derby Sunday finally dawns, strangely there is a calm air of expectancy out in the streets, like that before a storm or an election. When I wake and see my ticket on my bedside table, I feel butterflies in the pit of my stomach as if I myself were about to play.

The crowd plays an important role at the derby and gathers early, several hours before the start of the game. The area around the Olympic Stadium was originally a sporting forum built by Mussolini in the 1930s (see page 85 in the 'In the Footsteps of Fascism' chapter). Fans march in ant-like fashion over the shattered Fascist mosaics that line the walkways to the ground. The mosaics are inscribed with slogans such as '*Onore e Nemici*' ('Honour and Enemies') and overlooked by statues of young 'blackshirt' soldiers, all adding a bellicose tone to an already tense atmosphere around the stadium.

The police are out in force, and armed. Young officers on horseback look on nervously as a stone from nowhere bounces off an armoured van making a loud, hollow sound of the sort that often precedes violence here. The *carabinieri* funnel and frisk every fan through the turnstiles and into the ground, confiscating the caps from plastic bottles and the poles from banners. One year, apparently, police recovered chains and machetes branded with Nazi insignia, hidden in the surrounding hedges.

Reaching the top of the stairs that lead into the arena is like a minor conquest. It is for the spectator what walking out of the tunnel must be like for the players. Stretching before your eyes is the lush green grass of a pristine pitch, marked with clear white lines and encircled by a red running track. The arcing, white-ribbed roof of the crater-shaped stadium casts shadowed patterns on the pitch and defines a clear blue disc of sky. Seen in the distance through the roof, on the top of Monte Mario and flanked by cypress trees, a golden statue of an open-armed Christ presides over the secular deities of Totti, Batistuta and Nesta like a referee's spiritual assistant. Both ends of the stadium bulge and tremble with a colourful mass of fans, while the rows of expensive central seats, reserved for suited financiers, politicians and celebrities, no doubt still dining, take longer to fill.

Before kick-off in the afternoon the crowd is treated to a prolonged session of verbal foreplay, held between the opposing fans on the terraces. No blows are exchanged; like Don Quixote's war against the windmills, this superb duel is one of wits, confirming the Romans' penchant for a pasquinade. In this parallel match, in comparison to which the actual football match can seem just a banal sideshow, what counts is the originality of the message displayed on a banner.

Insults, jibes and fantastic claims painted in 2m-high letters are held up for the opposing fans to read 150m away at the other end of the ground. The spectacular choreography for the derby is carefully researched and prepared in the weeks preceding the game when both sides employ spies to ensure that each has ready-made responses to deflate their rival's taunts.

In the fiery red sea of the Curva Sud (Roma's end) a massive scroll is unfurled smothering many of the fans beneath. The Lazio fans at the other end of the ground read this giant, primitive form of a fax: '*Roma, alza gli occhi e guarda il cielo . . . è l'unica cosa più grande di te*', meaning 'Roma, raise your eyes and look to the sky . . . it is the only thing bigger than you.'

On the inside perimeter of the Curva Nord a group of hardcore 'Ultra' fans are assembling a response. They stand around a banner at strategic points, then hoist it up like a ship's mainsail: '*Infatti, il cielo è biancoazzuro*', 'Actually, the sky is blue and white' – Lazio's colours. A roar of approval ripples through the Curva Nord for Lazio's ironic goal.

Lazio in the past have scored highly with '*Se la Roma è magica, Cicciolina è vergine*', 'If Roma are magic then Cicciolina [a well-known pornstar] – is a virgin'. On another occasion, a clever play on words crafted from film titles stole the derby's terrace show: '*Con Boksic Instinct Lazio balla cui lupi*', or 'With Boksic [one of the club's star players] Instinct, Lazio dances with the wolves' – Roma's club symbol.

Meanwhile, Roma hits have included the self-explanatory 'Gazza fuck off', exhibited when the English star Paul Gascoigne played for Lazio; a huge silky tablet covering the entire Curva Sud inscribed with a poem in Latin declaring the historic rights of Roma to the city; the mildly amusing: 'Do your mothers know you are here?'; ten minutes of complete silence from the Roma fans while the

Laziali sang loudly: 'Be quiet, your breath smells'; and a sentimental favourite of the 1980s, a 50-square-metre white sheet that read simply: '*Ti Amo*' ('I love you').

One year Lazio raised a banner referring to Roma's laughable league performance and more particularly to its captain having been duped by a set-up on the TV show *Scherzi a Parte* ('*Joking Aside*'), with the wording: 'Keep cool, you're on *Joking Aside*'. The Curva Sud readily replied: 'Better a year on *Joking Aside* than eleven years on *Chi l'ho Visto*' – another popular TV show that searched for missing people, thereby referring to Lazio's prolonged spell in Serie B.

Of course, the visual spectacle counts in Italy. When the players walk out under the floodlights with their gelled-back hair and shiny red and blue kits the two ends of the ground erupt. Flags, bright flares and bangers create a cacophony of colour and noise. Ribboned balloons float up beyond the stadium's crater and for the first five minutes of the game the crowd is usually masked by a fog of coloured smoke.

Oh, and what about the match itself? When a goal is scored the celebration is volcanic and the crowd is gripped by a mass hysteria; colloquially a fan is called a *tifoso*, which literally translates as a 'carrier of typhus fever'. In recent years with both teams having painted the town in its respective colours after winning Lo Scudetto, the championship, for the first time in a generation, there have been some thrilling high-score encounters. But the public pressure on the players is so immense that the game is often a tense and scrappy affair, resulting in a low-score draw.

Still, if you happen to be in Rome on a derby weekend and manage to bag a prized ticket, forget computer generated simulation, this is the closest you will come to

experiencing how the crowds felt nearly two thousand
years ago when they watched the Reds against the Greens in
the circuses of Imperial Rome.

" Two things shaped my affair with Roman football and
both happened while I was teaching English after
hours to impeccably groomed bank managers at the
headquarters of the Banca Nazionale di Lavoro.

Firstly, a beginners' group, for whose kindness I feel
forever in debt, gave me a season ticket for one of the
city's two big clubs, Lazio. Secondly, I met 'Coca Cola',
a cleaner and leading fanatic of Lazio's rivals, Roma.

Like many people with only a rudimentary grasp of
each other's language, we struck up a friendship based
on football. Twice a week Coca Cola – whose real
name I never knew – would lean impatiently in the
doorway waiting for my lessons to end. When the
bankers had gone he would swagger into the classroom
and perch on the end of my desk. Then in his boyish
excitement he would slur his words while I struggled
to rescue footballing terms from his thick dialect.
Squat and dark with burnt chestnut eyes, he wore the
golden wolf's head pendant of Roma around his neck.

The first time he shifted his considerable bulk in my
direction he removed a wallet from his pocket, opened
it beneath my eyes and pointed proudly at a
membership card for one of Roma's most passionate
groups of supporters, the Commando Ultra Curva Sud
(CUCS). His membership number was 00002 and the
laminated card showed an explosive photo of twisted
red and yellow flags and flames. To the uninitiated it
was difficult to determine whether it depicted a scene

of intense jubilation or riot. 'I was there,' Coca Cola
said with a grin and an air of instigation.

I noticed that there were flames, too, on another
card in his wallet. It was the logo of Italy's neo-Fascist
party, what was then, in 1993, called the MSI. I
cautiously asked him how far he leant to the Right and
he jolted upright, thrust his arm out at a right angle to
his body and chanted 'MUSS-O-LINI.'

'*Pazzo*,' (crazy) said his fellow cleaner with a shake
of his head, while Coca Cola sniggered and his eyes
gleamed. He explained that at work and home he was
'*calmo, tranquillo*' but come the match on Sunday at the
stadium he was, he whispered in a foul breath – and at
this point drew his index finger across the width of his
neck and sucked hard on his cigarette – '*matto*'
(deemed a degree worse than *pazzo* on Italy's
unofficial hooligan scale). He laughed menacingly and
I laughed back, a little nervously.

As a lifelong Roma fan, Coca Cola recalled fondly
the memorable battles both on and off the pitch with
the ease of a good history teacher, and claimed that
Roma, unlike the rest of the league, had no amiable
twinning with other teams. As part of a sophisticated
network of national Ultra leaders – some of whom
are allegedly funded by the club – he claimed to know
who had stabbed whom on the morning of the 1985
Heysel Stadium disaster in Brussels in which 39 fans,
mainly Italians, lost their lives. While I wouldn't
want to bump into Coca Cola and his crew down
a half-lit alley wearing the wrong coloured scarf,
at this point he struck me as more of a gossip than
a warrior.

When I suggested as much his eyes widened and he stood up with an air of authority, rolled up his jumper and undid his belt, and gestured for me to feel the buckle. It was handmade and emblazoned with the head of a Roman centurion and a skull. Most surprisingly it was as heavy as a brick. He claimed that only last weekend he had run at a coach-load of Brescia fans and repeatedly thrashed the buckle against the coach window, cracking reinforced glass.

'Why "Coca Cola"?' I asked. After all, it wasn't an especially sinister nickname, though he pronounced it with the rasping sound of percolating coffee. Because, outnumbered and unarmed in a fracas with a mob of Inter Milan fans he had spied an empty Coke can, torn it in half and slashed one of the rival supporters.

I declined his offer to travel to an away game with Roma fans – the last time I'd travelled away in Italy with Verona fans we were herded by the army on to a chattel train and not allowed to leave the pack to buy food for an entire winter's day – but I agreed to join him at a home match. So we met at the Olympic Stadium, which Roma and Lazio share, each playing there on alternate Sundays.

Coca Cola stood at the foot of the terrace with his back to the goal. He was sweating and, like a demented director, yelling the first lines of songs to his band of teenage prodigies who wore crimson-and-gold silk bandannas around their foreheads. One of the factions of Roma fans was actually called the 'Boys', no doubt in homage to England's fearsome reputation in Italy for football violence. But in the well-segregated stadium it all seemed more boy-scout than anything else.

For all his bluster Coca Cola was an otherwise ordinary Roman – he also kept snapshots of his family in his wallet. Football gave him a grid in which to map out his life. Like hundreds of other Italian men he found an identity through quasi-religious worship of Roma, and in its opposition an outlet for the frustrations of a humdrum daily grind. This is occasionally expressed through violence but, thankfully, more often than not through a sort of ritualised pretence of violence.

Coca Cola hated the brash teams from the North, but he loathed Lazio even more. Little did he know as we stood beneath the Curva Sud that on this same terrace I stood and watched Lazio play every other weekend.

RELIGIOUS
ROME

AN AUDIENCE WITH THE POPE

Counting papal blessings

Seeing as pilgrims have been venturing to Rome from all corners of the world since the year dot, I thought the least I could do was to take a bus over to the Vatican and try to bag an invitation for the weekly papal audience.[1]

The word 'catholic' originates from the Greek for 'universal', and there are an estimated two billion Catholics in the world – the vast majority of whom come from the Americas and Europe, although there are sizeable contingents in the Philippines (52 million), India (14 million), Zaire (18 million) and Nigeria (10 million). Most Italians are of course nominally Catholic, though only about six million are practising.

The spiritual tourists, whose predecessors effectively spawned the travel industry in Rome, often travel in groups accompanied by the local priest. They come to visit the administrative and spiritual home of the Catholic Church, the Vatican City and St Peter's. The highlight of any such trip is to see the pope. Catholics have a frenzied familial concern for the pope, especially the current pontiff, John Paul II, who is fragile and visibly unwell.

On a Tuesday afternoon, after zig-zagging across St Peter's Square (Piazza San Pietro) several times as a result of skewed tourist-office directions, I found an untidy queue of about fifty people concealed beneath Bernini's pincer-like colonnade to the right of the square as you face the basilica. After half an hour or so among this anxious crowd – one family was arguing about who should go inside to collect their invites – it was my turn to climb the ramp leading up to bronze doors tended by two Swiss Guards. Passing beneath their pikes one has the strangest sensation of having gained access to a private and exclusive club. It's the same when you set foot anywhere in the tidy courtyards or sombre corridors of the Vatican excluding its church and museums. There's something ultra-historical about it, the complete contrary to theme-park history. This is real. Staff are clean cut, but to the imaginative their Armani suits and shades seem slightly sinister. I worried that at any moment someone might fling open a door and yank me inside for an inquisition.

When I reach the desk of the Prefettura della Casa Pontifica, two men dressed like hotel bellboys are dispensing invites from an alphabetically ordered box of envelopes. Thinking that I probably should have made a written application months in advance, I begin to explain . . . when I'm cast a 'save-your-breath' look and handed a blue invite. In swirly italics it reads: '*Udienza Generale Sua Santita Giovanni Paolo II*'. It's tomorrow at 10.30am. On the back of the papal card in five languages it simply states, 'This ticket is entirely free.' I felt grateful that the Vatican doesn't do things by halves.

I was genuinely surprised how straightforward it was to obtain an invite – for a private audience your local bishop has to make a written request, which can take months to be granted. I'd spent the whole of the previous day desperately scouring the city to find a ticket for the Roma *vs* Real Madrid football match, with no luck. (Well, not unless I'd been prepared to hand over a small fortune to an unsavoury tout.)

Despite what I'd read and heard from other people about the glutinous impenetrability of the Vatican, I was temporarily lulled into believing that perhaps some of the guards' famous Swiss efficiency contributed to it being an oasis in Rome's wider realm of red-tape nightmares.

The next morning no one even looks at my invite. I pass through airport style security screens supervised by armed *carabinieri* and then through modern gates to the left of the piazza. The faithful who have been queuing since dawn rush over the San Pietrini cobblestones – named after the hereditary workmen who for centuries have maintained the structure of St Peter's – to grab the best seats. On such a dazzling September morning, the polychromatic Swiss Guards could have been made for the cameras that snap them furiously. Groups with flags, pennants and instruments shuffle into the Piazza del Sant'Uffizio towards the Paul VI Audience Hall or Aula as it's known to the Vaticanisti.

Inside, the feeling of being in a school assembly is unavoidable. It's largely the effect of the hall, a sloping concrete space, built in 1970 by Pier Luigi Nervi, unadorned apart from a tangled web of bronze – a sculpture by Pericle Fazzini representing Christ having risen – that forms the backdrop to the raised stage. On the platform is an empty ivory upholstered chair not really grand enough to be called a throne.

The global crowd is in a carnival mood chanting and singing in anticipation of the big moment. The hall seats 6,500, but hundreds of us without allocated seating are left to fight for a view on the raised first-floor tier. It's like a rock-concert scrum at the back of the auditorium; booming German students sit on each other's shoulders while other pilgrims balance precariously on banisters. A party of elderly pilgrims threading rosary beads are shocked at how others are treating the sacred scene like a holy Disneyland. The best view for many is on the miniature screens of people holding video cameras high above their heads.

Flanked by two Swiss Guards with pikes and two bishops, and greeted by a volley of applause and flashbulbs, the Pope trundles to centre stage on an automated trolley that slides him on to his chair with the minimum of fuss. He acknowledges the faithful, now mostly hushed, with an agonisingly slow window cleaning action of his right hand. It reminds me of the raised hands of some of the statues of saints that oversee the roof of his church.

Amid the crowd and stuck at the back it's not easy to see much more than a hunched cream-white blob. But I have the Pope in my sights. My mini-binoculars quickly become hot property.

The Pope begins to read a brief sermon, the gist of which, I read in the next day's papers, is about world peace, followed by messages to the audience in four different languages. Often he speaks more. The messages are like radio requests. As he mentions the diocese and towns of each pocket of pilgrims in the audience they rise, tears in their eyes, and cries of '*El papa, viva el papa*' fill the auditorium. As each hears their pilgrimage blessed, an Austrian group dressed in lederhosen actually starts playing instruments and ringing bells, the Brazilian congregation performs salsa, and a band of Americans stand up, remove their hats and sing *God Bless America* in its entirety.

The Pope, though, is struggling. His voice is muffled and trembling, and fades in and out of earshot. Even in English it is difficult to follow complete sentences. Throughout his blessings he mops his brow and pauses to drink water. When he is not talking, his hands fidget and support either side of his head like the figure in Munch's ubiquitous portrait *The Scream*. It is as if the attention and ceremony are too much for him, and yet he has become the master at enduring boring ceremonies. Nevertheless, for a man in the advanced stages of Parkinson's disease, he looks well after the summer break. When the formalities are over he is swamped by people on stage each wishing to shake his trembling hand and give gifts.

The Pope may be ailing, but somehow seeing him in the flesh is like an antidote to some of the half-baked relics in the churches of Rome.

Here is a man who has created saints like they were going out of fashion and who follows a strident doctrinal line. Here is a man whose death will prompt all the church bells in Rome to ring simultaneously in his honour; a joyous sound on a solemn occasion, not heard since 1978 when they rang twice in one year. Here is a man whose role has an unbroken link to the last Roman emperors – and I am in awe of that but, as a non-Catholic, searching for religious significance amid the noise is a challenge.

On the walk back home over the Janiculum hill I stop at the smaller church of San Pietro in Montorio, built on the site where St Peter is wrongly presumed to have been martyred. In the church's cool, half light, beside Sebastiano del Piombo's *Flagellation*, I am grateful that there is always somewhere to gather one's thoughts in Rome.

1   Apply for free tickets to the Prefettura della Casa Pontificia, 06 6988 3273/3114, open 9am–1pm Mon & Weds to Sat, 3pm–8pm Tues.

THE
SWISS
GUARDS

Dressed to impress

In a city jam-packed with impressions of the past, the Swiss Guards are arguably Rome's greatest living anachronism. Resplendent in bulbous rooster-coloured uniforms inspired by the masters of Renaissance art they act as guardians to the gates of the Vatican's 44-hectare (109-acre) plot in the Eternal City. They are also the personal bodyguard to its most hallowed resident, Pope John Paul II.

The jester-style outfits of the guards, despite having been tweaked at the turn of last century, give the impression that in almost five hundred years since the private army was set up in 1506 by Pope Julius II, little has changed. But in recent years the Swiss Guards have had some thorny issues to contend with. The fallout from an alleged *ménage-à-trois* murder mystery in 1998 still rumbles on and there have been frequent reports by the world's press of a recruitment crisis and lack of leadership. At a time overwhelmingly characterised by daring terrorism, has the old guard run its course?

'Absolutely not,' affirms Corporal Tiziano Guarneri, a solid 28-year-old who has been with the guards for nine years. In the name of progress he explains how the recently departed commander of the guards, Pius Segmueller, employed Swiss military experts to reform the corps into a professional armed force. In May 2003 Segmueller also enrolled the guards' first non-white soldier, Dhani Bachmann, an Indian adopted by a German-speaking Swiss family at the age of five.

Given the Vatican's notorious impenetrability, particularly for foreign press, I feel somewhat privileged that Guarneri had painlessly agreed to an interview. No sooner am I past the Swiss Guards at the Porta Sant'Anna entrance to the Vatican, who are dressed in the more practical 'away strip' of blue cape and knee socks, than Guarneri appears with brusque Swiss efficiency – though, to my disappointment, he isn't in uniform.

Briefly, he shows me inside the barracks to a courtyard with stone benches and the flags of the 28 cantons of Switzerland hung across it. It feels enclosed like a prison. A couple of guards with their black pancake berets in their hands are checking the duty rota on a noticeboard. From the adjacent sports hall comes the echoing thud of a basketball.

I pursue my course: how, for example, would the guards respond to a close-range armed attack on the life of the pope of the sort that narrowly failed in 1981? 'We are each assigned very specific roles and a number. In a threatening situation the person on the left of the pope will have a different response from the person on his right,' says Guarneri. 'We are aware of each other's roles and keep in contact via microphones wired from our wrist.' The 2.5m halberds carried by the guards are largely ceremonial – but the men are also armed with discreetly concealed 9mm pistols.

Few jobs these days demand that you lay down your life for the sake of your employer. The guards' swearing-in oath – the *giuramento* – sets this sacrifice in stone. And not only the pope's life, but the lives of the entire College of Cardinals in the interim period – from when the bells of all the churches of Rome ring out in unison to mark the news of the pope's death to when the smoke signals emerge above Michelangelo's *duomo* to indicate that a new pope has been elected. Does such a high-profile security role not require the fitness and strategic nous of a paratrooper? 'Guards must have undergone at least preliminary training in the Swiss army and an intensive four-month course for new recruits,' says Guarneri. 'Personally I don't even have time to go to the gym. If a potentially serious situation arises adrenalin takes over. We know the routine and are very speedy.'

With a full quota of 110 guards, the regiment of Swiss Guards is not entirely alone in defending the world's smallest sovereign state. They are lent a hand by a 120-strong police force, the Vigilanza, who have had an increased presence in St Peter's since 11 September 2001. There are also the immaculately dressed young men in Armani suits and shades who patrol St Peter's church repelling those with exposed limbs; amazingly these are volunteer students from Rome's Catholic Gregorian University. A further cadre of plain clothes Swiss Guards accompany the pope on his travels.

One of the reasons for the recruitment crisis is the strict criteria for entry into the guards. Candidates for the obligatory two-year period of service have to be male, unmarried, physically and morally fit, under 25, at least 174cm tall and Roman Catholic. Switzerland, notably, is a predominantly Protestant country.

Earlier in the year Pius Segmueller had said: 'Part of the problem may be that we have very high standards and a tough selection process focused on quality not quantity.' But

Guarnerī says the problem has eased due to better advertising and recruitment campaigns within Switzerland.

Indeed it must be a very dull job at times, having to look so officious and disabusing tourists of their most unintelligible demands. Some of their questions beggar belief. 'Pardon me, but which way is the inquisition?' is one I've heard second-hand. And if urban myths are to be believed, it must be a frustrating job, too; one myth claims that female tourists throw their underwear and hotel keys to the guards (though no one in the Vatican would verify this).

In 1957 the writer HV Morton compared the guards to 'angry wasps'. I saw what he meant when I attended the Pope's weekly Wednesday morning audience. In the late summer warmth the guards' young faces beneath their black floppy hats changed from pink to scarlet as the scrabbling flock of papal fans pressed against them, while their ear sets, keeping them in radio contact with their colleagues, gave the impression they suffered from an epidemic of deafness. It must be hot beneath a uniform that has 109 separate pieces and was designed before the advent of central heating. As the ailing Pope, hunched and trembling, laboured through his multilingual blessings, the guards were repeatedly dazzled by flashbulbs – they are said to be the most photographed people in the world. Despite all the pressure and unwanted in-your-face attention, the young men had to remain patient. They could not 'sting' anyone.

'A Swiss Guard has something special inside of him – a combination of spirit and character. If he becomes frustrated by his public duties we pull him to one side and try to help out,' says Guarneri. Protecting the physical and spiritual well being of the court of the man who more than a billion people believe to be God's representative on earth is a serious business.

The guards work shifts of eight to eleven hours with breaks for meals cooked by nuns at the barracks. The starting salary – €1,048 – is perhaps a modest sum by Swiss standards, but as Segmueller says, with board and lodging included 'is not to be sniffed at here in Rome'. A system of curfews operates, graded according to age; for instance, on nights off the younger guards have to be back in their dormitory, alone, by midnight. After all, the multi-faceted, big-city charms of Rome must be a tempting new world to the fresh-faced recruits from the Swiss hinterland.

In the not-too-distant past there was a drunken late-night punch up between a group of guards and Italian police. In the end, peace had to be made by senior officials from both sides. Guarneri is candid: 'Sure problems of discipline occur, when some forget that we are the guards of the pope. We cannot be aggressive, but we have to know how to gain the upper hand.'

Much more injurious to the guards' holier-than-thou reputation has been the continuing saga of the deaths of the then newly appointed Commander of the Guard, Alois Estermann, his Venezuelan wife, Gladys, and 23-year-old Vice-Corporal Cedric Tornay. The three were found dead in the Estermanns' flat in the Vatican on 4 May 1998. The official Vatican report, published in February 1999, said that Tornay was ill and had murdered the couple before killing himself as an act of vengeance for not having been promoted.

It was not long before writers were expounding their own theories on the tragedy. There was talk of a gay affair between the two dead men, of an affair between the young man and Gladys who was a former model, of the commander's links to *Opus Dei*, a powerful, masonic Catholic organisation, and of a forged suicide note sent to Tornay's grieving mother, Madame Baudat, in Switzerland. Baudat was not impressed by the latter, and convinced of a cover-up insisted on a second post-mortem, which in 2003 concluded that her son had not committed suicide but had been murdered. The pathologist's report suggested that Tornay had been tied up and beaten unconscious before his death. Neither was there evidence that he had had a cyst on his brain as the Vatican had claimed.

Because the Vatican City holds special status as its own sovereign territory, it is unlikely that the mystery will ever shift beyond speculation to a satisfying judicial conclusion for people such as Baudat. If weathering controversial storms was an Olympic event, the Vatican would never be off the winner's rostrum.

The whole tragedy is definitely a no-go subject with Guarneri; it is old news and he prefers to focus on the present. Since Segmueller returned to Switzerland to become chief of police in his native Lucerne, Commander Elmar Mader has been in charge. He will be the guards' fourth commander in almost as many years – in their entire history there have been only about thirty commanders.

Most guards return to Switzerland after their two-year tour, but for others, like Guarneri, who decide to make a career in the guards the earthly rewards are auspicious. When he marries his Italian fiancée next month he will be provided with a family apartment within the Vatican – that's on top of the duty-free shopping, free medical care and full board.

For Guarneri, though, these perks pale beneath the mighty glow of history. He loves his work because every which way you turn in Rome history confronts you. It even courses through his private apartment. His rooms are based in a tower via which runs the famous *passetto*, a secret corridor connecting the Apostolic Palace to Castel Sant'Angelo. It was along here that Pope Clement VII was ushered to safety by the handful of Swiss Guards who hadn't been slaughtered by the invading troops of the Holy Roman Emperor Charles VI on 6 May 1527. The guards still observe the anniversary every year with a special ceremony.

According to the corporal his job satisfaction stems from being present where history is made. He has stood within hand-shaking range of such global luminaries as Queen Elizabeth II, Fidel Castro and George Bush during their respective meetings with the Holy Father. 'To be in the close presence of the pope and such guests is extraordinary. You can feel the love of the crowds towards the pope. I'm one in a hundred in the world and, yes, I'm proud of that.'

RELIGIOUS KITSCH

Sacred souvenirs

Only in Rome can an abundance of the sublime and the kitsch be found in such proximity. The Vatican City specialises in this sort of extreme contrast. One minute you can be admiring Michelangelo's *Pietà* in St Peter's basilica and the next be handling a nasty miniature copy available at one of the numerous religious souvenir shops that throng the holy territory. Throughout the inexhaustible Vatican Museums complex there are more than a dozen small boutiques strategically placed so that as soon as you've seen Raphael's *School of Athens*, you can buy the puzzle or the ashtray.

The museums' director argues that the upkeep and administration of such a bounteous art collection is cripplingly expensive and the shops help to generate income. He has a point. In an age where we've grown used to our culture being served up with coffee and posters only a fool would allow a captive audience of three million visitors a year — and that's just to the museums — to slip through the net.

Millions more indulge in the religious souvenir shops that encircle St Peter's Square. To secular tourists and perhaps to some believers, too, the commercial trade of sanctified images might seem distasteful and exploitative. But to many pilgrims these gaudy icons are seen as modern appropriations of holy relics. Don Ivor Parrish, a deacon studying at the English seminary college on Via del Monserrato, says religious mementoes are bought and used for purely devotional and contemplative reasons. Priests can often be seen buying copious quantities of spiritual knick-knacks to take back to their respective parishes and give them, or sell them, to their parishioners. And of course, concedes Don Parrish, one man's kitsch is another man's ideal.

But good taste comes at a price. The better stone or marble-dust busts of the Virgin Mary or the Apollo Belvedere, arguably hand-chiselled, start from €300. Beautiful all-wooden Christmas crèches, Vatican tapestries and jewel-embellished chalices run into thousands of euros. And because, for the faithful, Jesus, Mary, Padre Pio and John Paul II never go out of fashion, these shops never hold sales. The closest I have seen to a genuine discount was a sign saying: 'Buy six objects and only pay for five', a canny variation on the supermarkets' 3-for-2 offers.

In several outlets €18 will buy you a papal blessing, though only after your Catholicism has been verified by your parish priest. The certificates carry a photo of a younger, exuberant Pope John Paul II. But when the aged and ailing Holy Father goes up to heaven, these shops can expect their profits to go in the same direction.

After a liberal dose of serious art and austere churches, browsing in the souvenir shops is a welcome light relief. I saw an umbrella that opened up to create a mini St Peter's dome; a hologram of a bloody Christ on the cross, who was supposed to open and close his eyes but instead winked at me; a Christmas snow-shaker with a laughing pope who looked like Father Christmas; tacky models of friars swigging from flagons of wine and of nuns in sun-glasses playing cards; and hordes of plaster figurines scarred by the careless variations of mass production: a girthful Mother Teresa, a cross-eyed Mary and rows of grinning Jesuses (there's a word you don't often see in plural). The Vatican shops sold poker chips and golf balls, and although there wasn't a pope-on-a-rope soap in sight, they were offering a tasty line in Lolli-popes stamped with the face of His Holiness. Mercifully I didn't see any of the crassly sexualised tourist merchandise on sale elsewhere in Rome. Although as I write, holy knickers and dome-stamped bras are probably being produced in a factory in Naples.

Real flesh-and-blood nuns bustle around the shops filling plastic baskets with rosaries and crucifix trinkets. It's like being in one of those DIY bead shops. All purchases can be blessed and then sent on to your hotel.

On the brink of the mortal sin of despair, I wondered if there was anything affordable that's not mass produced. 'The Sistine Chapel 1,000-piece puzzle is good for the soul,' said an assistant at the Vatican Museum shop. And though it wasn't so good for my pocket, I bought it, but decided not to have it blessed.

ROME
AFTER DARK

BINGO!

Saturday night fever

Play the word-association game with Italy and it's not long before you come up with 'style' and its cognates. Think Versace, Ferrari and Marcello Mastroianni. Italians are born with an insouciance we can only dream of in Northern climes. They seem to know instinctively how to dress and where to be seen. As such, the latest *divertimento* that Romans are enjoying seven nights a week, and especially at the weekend, may come as a surprise. Instead of putting the world to rights between mouthfuls of silky truffles eaten from designer cutlery and casually parading the streets like a catwalk, droves of Italians are – wait for it – playing the sport of working-class grandmas, bingo.

But what's truly surprising is that it's not only the blue-rinse brigade playing. In Italy bingo has broken down age barriers. At the weekend swarms of Vespas are parked outside Rome's Bingo Re (Bingo King), a 3,000-square-metre bingo paradise ranged over two floors linked by escalators. Inside, twenty-somethings earnestly settle down to tick off random numbers in the hope of a cash injection. The ghost of Fellini would shudder at the demise of the *Dolce Vita*.

Bingo used to be called *tombola* in Italy. It was a popular game played by families after Christmas lunch and by pensioners using beans as counters at their local community clubs. Then, in 2000, in a drive to capitalise on the country's obsession with number games, the government legalised bingo as a commercial operation. Since then nearly 300 bingo halls have been opened and another 380 are due to be licensed soon. An Anglican church, a theatre and a castle are just some of the historic buildings that have been disembowelled for the pleasure of Italy's soft gamblers. A new bingo hall has even appeared at San Giovanni Rotondo, a little town in the South of Italy where pilgrims come to visit Santo Padre Pio's church. 'It's like opening a bingo club in Lourdes,' I'm told by Milena Gabanelli, a reporter for Italy's national RAI TV network, who made a documentary about bingo.

In Rome cinemas built half a century ago have been pillaged of seats and cheaply refitted with the fundamentals of the quick-fix bingo hall: video screens, tables, chairs, pots of felt-tip pens and a bingo-ball machine.

On a typical Saturday night at Bingo Re, players of all ages sit around tables smoking, while vendors, who double up as waiters, sell strips of bingo cards. At €1.50 a card it doesn't *seem* expensive, but some people play ten cards at a time, which is quite a feat given that the bingo caller scarcely breathes between numbers. Her robotic monotone has none of the chirpy Butlins bonhomie of cries of 'legs eleven' (cue wolf whistles), or 'Maggie's den, number ten' (cue hisses). She is under strict corporate orders that each game lasts no longer than ten minutes. Some are over in three minutes, making this the gaming equivalent of fast food.

In the short interval between games, tinny pop videos appear on screens around the hall and at the centre of each table. But come the time for eyes down, an uncanny silence – rarely found when Italians gather socially in public – settles over the hall.

A couple of well-Brylcreemed lads in muscle-hugging black T-shirts snigger when 69 is called. Then there is a cry of '*Piano!*' ('Slowly!') as a player struggles to keep up. A sleepy signora calls out '*Cinquina*' (a row of five) several numbers too late, and is jeered by the serious players who use thick fluorescent bingo markers brought from home. Other than these brief interruptions, and the occasional ring of a mobile phone, there is blanket quiet.

'In a way bingo is the new cinema,' says Paolo Fabrizi, a 24-year-old student. 'Sure, you have to concentrate, but it's cool. We come for a night out with friends and sometimes go home with a bonus.' The jackpot per game is about €250 on a typically busy night.

In response to the onslaught of bingo-mania, the Italian Cinema Agency, which has seen at least five cinemas in Rome recently close down, has voiced its concern about 'serious damage' to cinemas and the risk of 'cultural impoverishment' – a fate worse than death for many Romans, a number of whom still seem to live under the illusion that they are directly related to Caesar.

'How about a cultural version of bingo?' I suggest to a smart bank-manager type whose superstitious wife has moved to another table. 'When the caller calls out "Michelangelo" you have to identify the Sistine Chapel ceiling on the bingo card.' He looks bemused and remarks, 'The caller would have to go a lot slower.'

From the suited to the track-suited the brightly lit former supermarket is full of people from all walks of life. But what sort of people are they? 'Bingo attracts people with lots of time and few interests,' Fabio Bacchini, a sociologist at Rome's Eurispes research institute, tells me. 'Those who play bingo have neither faith in their own means nor in society and tend to rely on chance.' Worse still, he confirms that regular bingo sessions can lead to addiction.

Ominously, in the provinces the smaller bingo halls are not proving to be the Eldorado that the government had hoped for. As a result it is planning to introduce videopoker games and slot machines to the hard-up halls. For many Italians this is a step too far towards Las Vegas style operations, the likes of which Italy has always resisted.

'I'm worried about the old people,' the Archbishop Emeritus of Ravenna, Ersilio Tonini, told the Italian newspaper *La Republicca*. 'When they used to play cards in the *osteria*, they played in teams and used words and skill. With bingo there is only chance. Whoever approves of these bingo halls should read Dostoevsky to understand what remains of a man when he becomes a slave to chance.'

On my twelfth game at Bingo Re – I had intended to play only two – someone's hesitant shout of 'bingo' breaks the tense silence just as the ball that would have completed my card rolls on to the screens. I feel empty and glare in envy at the towering silver trophy on the winner's table. I get up to leave, but it isn't easy, especially after coming so close to the jackpot. The tension becomes electric after about fifty of the ninety balls have been called and the cry of 'bingo' is imminent.

On my way out I see an advert for bingo that reads: '*Vieni, Gioca, Vinci*' (Come, Play, Win), an unsubtle variation on Caesar's famous proclamation '*Veni, Vidi, Vici*'. I came and saw, but didn't conquer.

FORTE PRENESTINO

Going underground

A trip to the Forte Prenestino[1] in northeast Rome is a detour that few, if any, of Rome's millions of tourists ever make. Built in the early 1900s as an underground military base, the Forte Prenestino is a real fortress with a moat and drawbridge, but it is no longer an ammunitions base. Today, peace rules, man. Once it was impossible to locate the fort from the sky above, but nowadays, on a typical weekend evening it boasts outdoor cinema screens, concert lights and fireworks, for ironically it is now home to Rome's thriving subculture, the Centro Sociale. The surrounding area, Centocelle ('one hundred cells'), takes its name from the tunnels and cavernous rooms beneath it.

When the fort was beseiged on Labour Day, 1 May 1986, by two radical groups known as 'Lotta Continua' (the 'Fight Continues') and 'Gli Autonomi' ('The Independents'), no guns were fired – by this time the site had become merely an abandoned adventure playground. The takeover was part of a backlash among young Romans against consumerism, globalisation and corruption. Social centres boomed in the 1990s as abandoned buildings became occupied by squatters and transformed into cultural and political hubs, independent of both market and state control. Today, nearly a third are in Rome and Milan.

The Forte Prenestino remains the property of the Italian government, but since the siege it has continued to be occupied by the Centro Sociale Occupato Autogestito (literally, the 'Occupied Self-administered Social Centre'), a self-financing, self-governing body. It has no permits, doesn't pay taxes and works against all forms of bureaucracy. Its realm is the fort's 13 hectares (32 acres) of open, green space, the size and shape of a football stadium with hills at either end where fruit, vegetables and honey are cultivated.

The site is entered by an imposing moat gate and is criss-crossed by tunnels decorated with anti-establishment murals. In Italy it is the only structure of its kind occupied by civilians, open to the public, and offering a range of activities. Entrance is on a pay-what-you-can-afford basis. As well as concerts and films the fort hosts a recording room, a gym, a tattoo and piercing studio for the latest in body art and a natural cosmetics shop full of home-grown products. The bookshop sells publications by La Stampa Alternativa, one of Italy's anarchist publishers, and a canteen serves wholesome home-made food. All the facilities are run and staffed, unpaid, by the fort's residents.

The fort is a meeting place and home for students, travellers, members of the 'No Globals' environmental campaign, artists, musicians and families that seek an alternative environment. The community of fifty or so people live in garage-like squats built into the side of the fort. Its atmosphere is like that of Glastonbury Festival but without the headliners and the tents. Several of Italy's better-known underground bands started out on the fort's low-cost stage, such as 99 Posse, who went on to produce the visceral rap music for Gabriele Salvatores's 1993 film *Sud*, and the global rocker Manu Chao. 'Each time you come here you make new friends and discover a previously unfound zone. It sounds like a tall order, but you may even discover a new way of understanding the world,' says one regular wearing super-baggy trousers and rolling a joint.

So how is life at the fort different from the world beyond the bunker's walls? Dora, whose long dreadlocks and military outfits complement her combative personality, gave up her apartment and office job ten years ago for life 'inside' the fort. She runs the cinema and says she relishes the fort's lifestyle of 'no conflict, honest dialogue, its concentration of positive energy and its desire to be productive.'

But Maurizio, a chirpy, organisational whizzkid who was one of the original occupants and founders of the fort complex, thinks that the centre has become saturated with events and ideas and it's a good time to reflect on its direction. He goes on to describe how it works: 'To become part of the organisation or to promote your own activity all you have to do is frequent the place, get to know us and then participate at our meetings.' If the newcomer's idea is coherent to the fort's philosophy – 'the desire to be free from the chains of society and governments' – then it becomes part of the programme.

In the daytime the surrounding park offers activities for children, but late at night its handful of bars open and the fort transforms. Punkish music and hippified chill-out zones may not be to everyone's taste, but it gives a rare flavour of the previous generation's turn-on, tune-in and drop-out lifestyle. And it sure beats the hassle of trying to find a parking space in Trastevere at the weekend, with its

tiresome queues, formal membership cards and costly
cocktails.

1   FORTE PRENESTINO, Via F Delpino a Centocelle, 06 2180 7855,
     www.forteprenestino.net. The fortress can be reached by trams no.
     14, 19 and 516.

VESPERS AT SANT'ANSELMO

A quiet night out

There are few parts of modern central Rome untouched by a bus route. The Aventine hill, with its orange groves, ancient churches and luxury villas, is one such haven. The only tourists who breach its summit are dropped off by tour buses to peek through the 'holy' keyhole at the gate of the Priory of the Knights of Malta, or Villa Magistrale dei Cavalieri di Malta. Through it you can see three sovereign territories: that of the aristocratic Knights of Malta, which has its own head of state and passports, Italy and the Vatican.

Across the Maltese square – a curious cul-de-sac designed by Gian Battista Piranesi in the eighteenth century, and where the *carabinieri* keep a full-time watch – is another retreat, the church of Sant'Anselmo. Its driveway leads to a courtyard adjoined by a college of philosophy and theology, and the cells of its Benedictine order of monks. All year round the view to the right of the courtyard is remarkable for any city centre: it resembles a shimmering jungle out of which rises a distant medieval church façade like a lost temple above the foliage.

The church of Sant'Anselmo, built by Francesco Vespignani, son of the famous Roman architect Virginio Vespignani, in 1893, is a mere *bambina* compared with its elegant fifth-century neighbour, Santa Sabina. Its interior décor is refreshingly unadorned, with rows of shiny Doric columns and stained-glass porthole windows set high in magnolia walls. When the candles are lit the ambience is positively bistro-like, making Sant'Anselmo the perfect setting for a quiet night out in Rome.

Try to arrive early enough to catch the adjacent shop open. Run by the resident brotherhood it sells liqueurs and chocolate made at monasteries and nunneries throughout Italy. Invest in a bottle and a bar, or several, as the money goes to a worthy cause.

At 7.15pm on most Sundays and national holidays about fifty monks, heads bowed in black and brown hooded robes, file in from the college to the church. They divide into two sections filling the pews either side of the altar. The priest and his team of two, all three wearing white gowns threaded with golden veins, take to the high altar.

The soft chants begin. It is a strangely distant yet familiar sound – collections of Gregorian chants have been bestsellers in recent years. Heard live, the whole experience is enriched by the atmosphere of the church, filled with shadows and incense spices. The synchronised bowing and the swinging of the burners in time to the chants become quite hypnotic. Of course it's in Latin, but don't let that hinder your enjoyment. Unless you're an ancient language specialist, it's the tonal harmony that counts. The chants possess a penetrating, meditative quality; the whole scene an air of *The Name of the Rose* mystery.

'Vespers is a spiritual boost without having to sit through an often leaden and impregnable Catholic mass,' says a regular visitor. 'It offers a break from the secular urban rush. You can feel the chants recharging your batteries. What's more, it's a fine time to savour the church interior. So many churches are overlooked in Rome.'

Sandal-clad monks going about their business are a fairly common sight in downtown Rome, but there's an added poignancy seeing them gathered en masse in worship. There is no star performer or greatest hit, just a satisfying constancy. The graceful movements of the priest are the very antithesis of pop-music choreography. As the vespers end and the monks shuffle away, turning to genuflect as they leave, there is complete silence. Then darkness falls as the last brother to leave extinguishes the candles.

In fact, it's so quiet you can hear your tummy gurgle. Now you should be ready to appreciate the liqueur and chocolate!

MAGICAL ROME

Mystery tours and fortune-tellers

While Harry Potter has brought about a universal revival in all things wizardy over the past few years, magic has always been a salient feature of Italian society. Ample listings of wizards, witches, faith healers and pranotherapists in the Rome phone book prove that demand for mystic contact remains high, continuing a tradition of soothsayers as popular oracles that dates from the days of ancient and medieval Rome. Indeed, a study conducted in 2001 concluded that 17 per cent of the Italian population was involved in astrology, magic and occultism. Like yoga and the gym, the medium of magic has become a lifestyle habit, fuelled by the Italians' lingering weakness for superstition and the supernatural.

A theology college in Rome runs courses exploring mysticism and its links with religion, and academics have posited the thesis that the occult has filled the vacuum left by the demise in church attendance. Yet a Salesian priest from Turin, Don Silvio Mantelli, who uses magic tricks to entertain his parish, recently petitioned the Vatican for a patron saint of conjurers, magicians and wizards. Taking a magic wand as a gift for the Holy Father, he said that the Pope told him: 'You'll need a lot of magic wands to change our world; but let's make a start with this one.'

Don Mantelli is optimistic that his proposal will be accepted and, hey presto, will make the nineteenth-century Italian priest San Giovanni Bosco the official patron saint of magic. As a trainee priest Bosco used to baffle his fellow students by making a plate of steaming pasta disappear in one house and reappear in another and by making red or white wine flow from the same bottle at will. He quickly became a crowd puller and learned to use his magic to convey his religious message. Following his founder's example, Don Silvio has travelled all over the world giving performances billed as the 'Wizard Sales'.

You may not catch Don Silvio 'performing' in Rome, but for those wishing to see how magic is woven into the city's streets, Professor Roberto Quarta has been running magical mystery tours[1] within the historic centre for eight years. His range of walks includes the Ghosts of Rome and Mysterious Shadows on Ponte Sisto, and one called Magic, Alchemy and Esoteric Rome which – starting from Piazza Navona, passing through Campo de' Fiori and moving on to Ponte Sisto – concentrates on characters of the Middle Ages and Counter-Reformation. These include Giordano Bruno and Beatrice Cenci, who were both accused by the authorities of involvement in witchery of sorts and both met gruesome ends.

Meanwhile, the colonnaded arcade of Galleria Colonna, which is directly opposite Piazza Colonna on Via del Corso, is permanently occupied by a number of fortune-tellers and tarot-card readers. Most of them offer a service in Italian or English. While no one can guarantee what the future holds, these fortune-tellers do at least provide a reply, which is more than La Bocca della Verità ever gives. The 'Mouth of Truth', an ancient drain cover

housed in the porch of the church of Santa Maria in
Cosmedin, was made famous by the scene in *Roman
Holiday* in which Gregory Peck and Audrey Hepburn take
this litmus test for liars.

Street-entertainers and magicians of fluctuating
talent give regular performances around the main tourist
nightspots, especially Piazza Navona and Campo de' Fiori.
Of all these acts, one magician deserves a special mention.
Known and adored by locals and tourists alike, 'Il Mago' of
Rome is a big hit – not so much for his magical talent as for
his notoriously bad tricks and Oscar-worthy performances.
Assisted by his 'magic bone' he serves up ludicrous tricks
with the formality of a head waiter, his face contorted in
fake pain. But when he skewers his neck with a sword or
guillotines his fingers the audience's squeals of laughter (not
horror) can be heard several blocks away. So make sure you
keep your ears open for Il Mago's famous catchphrase:
'*Guarda uno, guarda due, guarda tre*' ('Watch one, watch two,
watch three'). Especially if you're a Harry Potter acolyte.

1   ESOTERIC WALKING TOURS, 192 Viale Regina Margherita, 06
        8530 1758, e-mail ilsogno@romeguide.it. Walks cost €42 for two
        people and run most nights at 9pm; it's recommended to book in
        advance and request an English-speaking guide.

HIP HOTELS

The most stylish places to stay

For years the hotel scene in Rome was more 'hip replace-
ment' than hip. Blessed with a ceaseless tide of cultural and
religious pilgrims, aged hoteliers became content to rest on
their laurels. Invariably their hotels would be in a choice
location, perhaps housed in an old villa or a convent, but the
buildings lacked imagination and charm.

Now, however, it is *so* last century to stay at a hotel
where a gummy-eyed porter nods you in the direction of an
airless room laden with gloomy cast-off family furniture.
Blazing the trail are a few studiously revamped hotels that
have mimicked aspects of the so-called boutique hotels of
other major capitals to produce designer Roman accommodation. And because the city is so wedded to its historical
tradition, the results are all the more impressive.

Like many lodgings of pedigree, Hotel de Russie[1] on
Via del Babuino is in an enviable spot, in the heart of the
stylish shopping district with views over sun-swept Piazza
del Popolo. Russian dignitaries stayed here in the nineteenth
century, and while Picasso was in residence with the
Russian National Ballet he is said to have picked oranges
from his window. World War II brought an end to the

building's function as a hotel and it was used as the head-quarters of Italian state television, RAI, until 1993. In the late 1990s it was restored to its original purpose and opened as one of Rocco Forte's flagship luxury hotels in 2000.

Inside, the German architect and designer Tommaso Ziffer has fused elegance with modernity taking Rome of the 1930s and 1940s as his inspiration. In the sleek paired lobbies that flank the entrance hall, chic high-back sofas and wrought iron chandeliers are juxtaposed with modern sculpture. The homely rooms have soothing sugared-almond pastel walls hung with radiant photographs of flowers (not the usual reproductions of period prints) and are furnished eclectically. References to antique Rome are restricted to copies of sea-faring mosaics in the marble bathrooms. By locals' standards it qualifies as 'minimal', but 'pared down in a Roman way' would be a more accurate description – in the crucible of hip and trendy, Rome is a slow burner.

The highlight of the hotel, and worth visiting even if you can't afford its five-star prices, is the spectacular terraced garden. The former vineyard laid out by Valadier is now brimful of mighty evergreens, rose bushes and citrus trees, and at night hundreds of candles infuse it with a magical incandescence. Johnny Depp and Leonardo DiCaprio are known to burn the midnight oil in the Stravinsky bar – the composer had a favourite suite – when they stay here. But perhaps a truer mark of Hotel de Russie's success is the Roman cognoscenti who gather here for lunch or dinner.

Across Piazza del Popolo from Hotel de Russie is Hotel Locarno.[2] The formerly frumpy Locarno recently expanded into an adjacent building that once housed a bank.

Its spacious, historic rooms have ultra-high ceilings, parquet and marble floors, lots of neoclassical detail and are crammed with antiques bought at auction. The restored pre-war bathrooms are a treat. In keeping with the clean-up of traffic and pollution in the area, the hotel provides bicycles for guests.

But by far the hippest hotel in Rome, and the only one to write its name in lower case, is the ripa hotel[3] in Trastevere. A hotel since 1973, but restyled in 1998 by the Roselli and King studio, the award-winning ripa has maintained its original façade but styled its contemporary designer interiors on themes of transparency and light. Its 170 Manhattan loft-style rooms make artful use of space. There is no wardrobe (as your Prada trainers and Paul Smith suits are a personality signature that should be out on display), the minibar has been wrapped in black felt and suspended, and the bubble TV sits on a disc of stainless steel on a black chaise longue. A pebble-patterned carpet and Barbarella bathroom complete the picture. Guests are sorted for food and entertainment, too, as the ripa is home to one of Rome's most popular rave venues, Suite, and the Riparte cafe serves food grown on the proprietor's farm. Clearly this is not aimed at the traditional Romans who grumbled about the contemporary touches at Hotel de Russie, but at weekend jetsetters who like to travel in style.

1   HOTEL DE RUSSIE, 9 Via del Babuino, 06 328 881,
      www.roccofortehotels.com. Double rooms cost €360 to €620.
2   HOTEL LOCARNO, 22 Via della Penna, 06 361 0841,
      www.hotellocarno.com. Double rooms cost €190 to €200.
3   RIPA HOTEL, 1 Via Orti di Trastevere, 06 58 611,
      www.ripahotel.com. Double rooms cost €165 to €250.

" The seventeenth-century seaside villa La Posta Vecchia
(The Old Post House; Palo Laziale, Ladispoli, Rome,
06 994 9501, www.lapostavecchia.com) is a panacea,
especially for those who insist on visiting Rome in
midsummer when the city can feel like a pressure
cooker. On the coast northwest of Rome – forty
minutes away by road or train – the former post
house immortalised in a painting by Gaspar van
Wittel, and once home to the billionaire John Paul
Getty, is like a multi-starred *agriturismo*, with rooms
costing from €320. It is beautifully situated in its own
manicured grounds complete with a private beach,
covered swimming pool and views of a castle. Each
suite boasts its own historic character, and there's an
almost obscene ratio of 44 staff to 38 beds.

For Getty, who preferred wheels to wings, it was a
stopover on the drive between his home in Zurich and
his oil-well hobby in southern Italy. Once the tycoon
had persuaded Prince Odescalchi, who also owned
the castle next door, to sell him the pile, it was
restored by a team of ninety (including four
architects) during the mid-1960s.

With the help of Professor Federico Zeri, the
curator at the time of the Getty Museum in California,
Getty began to collect fine antiques and art works to
decorate the villa. Much of the furniture is from
eighteenth-century Tuscan and Umbrian churches.

For about a decade La Posta Vecchia became a
deluxe drop-in centre for Getty's friends and hangers-
on. Famously parsimonious, he installed public
phones for his guests, some of whom had been
clocking up hefty phone bills calling America. 'If you

want a pool, you pay for it,' he told his lady
companion Madame Tissier (according to the hotel
manager), and that's exactly what she did. In true
control-freak style the door between their adjoining
suites only opened from his side.

Getty left Italy in 1975 following his grandson's
brutal kidnapping there. However, when the villa
changed hands in the early 1980s, every detail
remained exactly as Getty had left it.

Every room has its own individual style. The Medici
suite is dominated by a gilded bed made from a
seventeenth-century baptistry, with a headboard
upholstered in turquoise velvet. Through a door an
elegant stairwell leads down to a rosy antique-marble
bathtub set in front of an open fireplace – with the
windows and shutters open one can hear the gentle
lapping of the sea. Maria de' Medici's carved dowry
chest was removed from the suite, however, after guests
complained that it felt like they were sleeping with a
sarcophagus; the offending object is now in the salon.

A tapestry threaded with gold hangs in the Getty
suite, which is furnished with period pieces in carved
and polished oak. Downstairs in the restaurant a
communal table overlooking the sea was made from
Roman columns of Numidian marble hauled over
from Turkey. Wealthy as he was, it's amazing Getty
was allowed to cut the precious pillars for his
domestic pleasure.

During the excavations for a swimming pool
beneath the hotel, two Roman villas dating back to
the second century BC were unearthed (the pool was
instead built on the terrace). One of the villas might

even have belonged to Tiberius, who along with Julius
Caesar is known to have had a sumptuous summer
bolt-hole along the same coast. When I visited, a
group of local amateur archaeologists, who tend to
the subterranean site, were sifting through fragments
like a giant puzzle to complete a mosaic.

'This place has enough history to keep the
conversation buoyant between even the most jaded of
honeymooners,' jokes the manager. At more than
€1,000 a night for the master suites you'd expect
nothing less than your own private museum.
Fortunately, guided visits are arranged for the
plebeian public by appointment on Tuesday
afternoons.

BED &
BREAKFAST

At home with the Romans

In order to obviate the crush on Rome's hotels during the Jubilee year the city came up with a smart idea. Families with spare rooms could spruce them up and offer them to tourists on a Bed & Breakfast basis. As a result there are now several hundred homely bases throughout the city available for visitors. They are reasonably priced, flexible and afford an opportunity to see what goes on behind the shutters in a Roman's home.

If it's an Italian experience you seek, then this is inside-track accommodation. It is not uncommon for hosts to lavish on you edible treats, insider information on the neighbourhood and rants on the state of the nation (I've received entire papal histories while politely watching reruns of *Miss Italy* over coffee and brioche).

On top of this there's a desire to make you feel at home rarely found in budget hotels. I've found that some hosts will go to great lengths to rustle up a full English breakfast, believing that we all trot off to work with a stomach full of bacon and eggs – maybe because B&B has connotations of Britishness, many host families express an eager curiosity for British idiosyncrasies.

This being Italy, hygiene is paramount. Technically the hosts aren't allowed to handle any foodstuff that they serve you. Health and safety rules state that breakfast should be pre-packed, but, mercifully, I've found that Italian hosts can't bear to be restricted by such killjoy red tape. I've woken up to the aroma of cakes being baked, been served home-made limoncello indecently early in the morning and even been invited to the family evening supper.

Some B&Bs are no more than extensions of small hotels – which may serve a purpose, but lack the personal welcome. Many have websites that are worth browsing before booking. It is advisable to e-mail or telephone beforehand to check that they meet all your requirements, for example whether you may have to share a bathroom with the owner and/or other guests.

I have stayed in three B&Bs that I'm happy to recommend to friends visiting Rome. The first is Campofiori B&B,[1] the home of Giuseppe Conte – a suave and mellow man of a distinguished age – located in a hazardously cobbled lane just off Campo de' Fiori. The alley, once lined with craftsmen's workshops, now sports a deluxe pet shop and a gym. According to Giuseppe, who gets the goods in for breakfast from the superb bakeries and *alimentari* around the Campo, this part of Rome still retains vestiges of village life. Perfectly poised between the centre and Trastevere, Campofiori B&B exemplifies the way that people live so close together in central Rome, where space is at a premium.

'This was probably once the home of a cardinal,' says Giuseppe. It's a cosy set-up; the guest room is full of chunky history and art books and its high ceiling has original chestnut beams and restored family etchings from the seventeenth century. Literally within spitting distance, Trattoria

Da Sergio offers hearty Roman fare. But if you're prepared to explore further afield, Giuseppe has a list of his favourite Roman restaurants. At no extra cost he will polish your shoes, and he always carries his guests' luggage to the taxi rank. And if like me you forget to bring a toothbrush, he has spares that he has garnered from hotels on his own travels.

La Rampa B&B[2] has a fabulous location in the corner of the Piazza Trinità dei Monti at the top of the Spanish Steps. The nineteenth-century building is named after the Rampa Mignatelli, a rather hidden alternative ascent to the Pincian hill from Piazza di Spagna, and guests have the keys to both of the building's entrances – one at the foot and one at the top of the ramp. The exclusive Hassler Hotel lies opposite, and the Villa Borghese and Spanish Steps are on its doorstep. Around the corner at no. 22 in the square below, there's the colossal cast of a Roman bust in the courtyard.

The owner Anna Manieri is well suited to her grandiose surrounds. For many years she owned her own fashion shop in the piazza and organised catwalk shows at the soon-to-be-restored Casina Valadier mansion on the Pincian hill. The immediate area is a fashion nerve centre. Downstairs is the headquarters of Mariella Burani (who Anna assures me is a big league designer), and from one of the bedroom windows you can see Valentino's workshop. The swashbuckling poet Gabriele D'Annunzio lived in the house for a year, and Anna jokes that a night here will leave you with a fiery spirit and a poet's tongue.

There's a glamorous Hollywood feel to the apartment's décor. The two double rooms, each with their own immaculate marble bathroom, open on to a living space with a giant circular mirror. But there's no such thing as a wafer-thin film-star's diet here. Breakfast, taken in the antique side of the flat, consists of chocolate cake, *cornetti* and peeled fresh fruit, and Anna even cooks bacon and eggs for some of her regular guests.

Finally, for a panorama from one of the Roman film director Nanni Moretti's favourite parts of town – Monteverde Vecchio – try B&B Gianicolo.[3] It's a roomy apartment on the fourth floor of a 1920s building on Rome's eighth hill, the Janiculum (or Gianicolo), in a leafy, genteel neighbourhood. There's a bus stop right outside, but it's only a short walk down the hill into Trastevere and a slightly longer walk to St Peter's. The highlight of a stay at Signora Gabriela Pisani's house is breakfast served on a sun-dappled roof terrace. The view from here, and from all the rooms, is breathtaking.

Signora Pisani is an enterprising woman full of practical tips on how to make the most of your stay in Rome. She even offers a three-day cookery course should the luscious smells from her kitchen tempt you; call the B&B for details. (Or for an in-depth five-day cookery course, see the chapter 'Diane Seed's Roman Kitchen', page 17).

For a full list of B&Bs in Rome, visit one of the city's tourist information points and pick up a free copy of *Guida ai B&B di Roma*, published by Promonet and the Rome tourist office. Alternatively, request one directly from the tourist office (5 Via Parigi, 06 3600 4399).

1   CAMPOFIORI B&B, 20 Vicolo delle Grotte, 06 679 5939, e-mail g.conte@promedinternational.com. One double room from €60.
2   LA RAMPA B&B, 16 Piazza Trinità dei Monti, 06 6794288, e-mail bed&breakfast16@hotmail.com, Two doubles from €110 each.
3   B&B GIANICOLO, 11 Via Nicola Fabrizi, 33 9339 6026, www.bbgianicolo.com. Three double rooms from €110 each.

ONE NIGHT WITH KEATS

A Romantic's retreat

The apartment on Piazza di Spagna where John Keats once lived is now run by the Landmark Trust and rented out as a holiday home. It is in the same block as the Keats-Shelley House museum,[1] and is decorated and furnished in early nineteenth-century style with engravings of Rome and sketches of Keats. Known as the 'Casa Rossa' because it was the only pink house in the paintbox-coloured square, its mod cons include a modern kitchen, a power shower and double glazing on the two bedroom windows, which helps to keep out the noise from the crowds that gather each night on the Spanish Steps.

In the living room there is a small but excellent selection of books about Rome, in addition to well-thumbed copies of the collected works of John Keats. The view out is towards the obelisk and two cupolas of the church of the Trinità dei Monti that crowns the top of the famous rococo stairway.

The flat's smallest bedroom has been restored to how it would have looked in the Romantic poet's final three months from November 1820. Located directly above the one in the museum that Keats rented for £21 per week, it is a sparsely furnished narrow room with honeycomb russet tiles, a marble fireplace and a desk. As he lay on his bed the delirious Keats must have seen swirling patterns in the floral latticed ceiling where the motifs look like Roman rosetta bread rolls.

Rome's relics had worked miracles for many, but neither the bones of saints nor its salubrious climate could save Keats. He seemed stained by death. As a teenager he had dissected corpses as part of his training to become a surgeon, and by the age of 23 he had lost both his parents and seen his beloved brother die in his arms. In his diary (which can be seen in the museum) in February 1821, his friend Joseph Severn records that Keats, having not slept for nine days, 'is a broken man.' And then simply: 'He is gone – he died with the most perfect ease – he seemed to go to sleep.'

But the poet's outer calm concealed the physical damage that tuberculosis had wreaked on his body. When a doctor opened up his chest, 'the lungs were completely gone,' wrote Severn. The next day his death mask was cast; it is now on display in the museum. After his death Keats's bedroom furniture was burnt in the piazza (perhaps out of superstition or for health precautions), causing Severn to exclaim with rage: 'Those brutal Italians.'

The night I stayed in the house where Keats died was Halloween. The following day, 1 November, is called the Giornata dei Defunti ('Day of the Dead') when Italians visit the cemeteries where their deceased loved ones rest. Not having any family buried in Rome I planned to visit Keats's gravestone at the Protestant Cemetery (see page 133).

That's if I made it through the night – it was not turning out to be one of 'mists and mellow fruitfulness' as described in Keats's *Ode to Autumn*. Around midnight the skies rumbled and cracked open, hurling down bolts of lightning. The ominous claps of thunder seemed to shake the house and echoed the tremors of an earthquake that had registered earlier in the day in Rome. I read Keats's odes, and when the lights went off unexpectedly I read them by candlelight. In true Gothic style I faintly hoped that his ghost would show up.

The apartment allows you to take a step back into history, but had Keats's spirit appeared that night what would he have made of the scene outside? He might have recognised the sound of the horse-drawn cabs that beat over the cobblestones in the morning and the lone chestnut vendor at the corner of Via Condotti with his pile of sacks and tin drum of burning coals. The exterior of the palazzo would have been familiar to him, too. It has been restored as closely as possible to its original nutty vanilla colour on the first two levels and a sandy orange on the third and fourth tiers with chocolate brown shutters. In this respect the Eternal City grows younger every day. But what about the water cannon washing down the Steps late at night, or the risqué Benetton advert covering the façade of the palazzo opposite like a giant blind?

As for the square being a tourist magnet, Piazza di Spagna was already known as the English Ghetto by the time Keats arrived (see the chapter 'Babington's Tea Rooms', page 27). In 1815 a Reverend Robert Finch stayed at no. 26, where Keats would later reside, when it had just opened as lodgings. It seems as though Finch had more than just herds of tourists to contend with. 'I shall adopt the plan of breakfasting at home which is convenient, as a flock of goats comes to the steps of my door every morning,' he said, in praise of this early form of organic food delivery.

The morning after my fairly sleepless night the city was dead except for clusters of tourists under umbrellas. The rain was pounding down and a serpentine stream wound its way down the empty steps to the bottom where the Barcaccia fountain – which records the arrival of a boat in the piazza after the Tiber flooded the city centre in 1598 – frothed like a Jacuzzi.

The only signs of commercial life were the florist's stall and Bangladeshi hawkers selling stubby umbrellas from doorways. Keats hadn't shown up for me, so I bought a flower and made my way across the city to the Protestant Cemetery. A handwritten note on the gate announced that it was closed due to flooding. A cemetery closed on the Day of the Dead? It could only happen in Rome.

1   THE KEATS-SHELLEY HOUSE, 26 Piazza di Spagna, 06 678 4235, www.keats-shelley-house.org. The Keats apartment at the same address sleeps four and is booked through the Landmark Trust in the UK, 01628 825925, www.landmarktrust.co.uk, from £239 per night, minimum of three nights.

" The several leather-bound guest books at Keats's apartment make for an engrossing read. Most comments are laudatory, but there's a fair smattering of gripes about the noise from the Spanish Steps. Some entries are twenty pages long; some are fluent, some rambling; others are more scientific, using coded diagrams to explain how the newly installed air-conditioning system works.

A sojourn at the poet's former flat seems to stir guests to find their muse – usually in the form of Rome – and pen ditties. Be warned: the poetry is not up to the Romantics' grade. There are rhymes about

'treats' and 'Keats', silly verses about the socks of
Shelley being smelly and no shortage of lines about
the babble from the piazza below: 'We just don't care
if we can't sleep/This after all is the heart of
Rome/And we can sleep when we get home.'

Some guests leave fascinating personal tips: 'Near
the birthplace of the exiled Stuarts, Charles the Young
Pretender and his brother Henry, Stuart shortbread is
baked at the church of Santi Apostoli and sold from a
stall beneath the portico.' While others are just plain
funny: 'Women shopping on the fashionable Via
Condotti should be aware of the very strict dress
code: shoulders, arms and legs should be *uncovered*.'
And witty: 'Most surprising sight of the week was a
couple on a scooter wearing crash helmets.'

True to English character there are those who
use the guest book to express one-upmanship.
When Keats didn't want to cook on his fireplace
stove he had his meals sent up from what used to be
the humble Trattoria Lepri opposite Café Greco.
One couple, however, record how they had their
dinner sent down from the five-star Hassler Hotel
at the top of the Steps. Which sure beats pizza
delivery, even in Italy.

In just one week another couple record that they
witnessed no fewer than three film shoots and six
wedding photo sessions from the flat's enviable
vantage point. But that's just an ordinary day in the
life of the Spanish Steps. For those guests lucky
enough to be in residence around midsummer, the
apartment offers a bird's-eye view of the annual
fashion parade as its models sweep down the carpeted

steps: 'Had VIP window view of Naomi and co as they strutted their stuff for the paparazzi,' reads one early July entry. It's also a prime location for the Feast of the Immaculate Conception on 8 December: 'Pope drove past our front door in his mobile car.' Now that doesn't happen at home.

CHILDREN'S
ROME

TIME
ELEVATOR
ROMA

A leap back in time

Weaving through the crowds of shoppers along Via del
Corso I am accosted. Bizarrely, it is in almost the exact same
spot, opposite Palazzo Doria Pamphilj, where I was last
assaulted. On that occasion it was gypsy children thrusting
a sheet of cardboard horizontally above my waist while they
tried to rifle through my pockets – a humiliating experience
for someone who counts his time spent in Rome in years
not days. This time the tool is a knife held to my throat, but
as I turn my head slowly to see who is wielding the weapon,
I realise that it too is made from cardboard and my assailant
is a grinning schoolboy.

With his black hair brushed forward like an
emperor's and wearing a loose white tunic and sandals, he
looks as though he has just stepped out of a Caravaggio
canvas (his sunglasses, however, confirm my grip on the
present). His sidekick is a much older man who he says is a
gladiator, but whose fancy dress is clearly that of a Roman
centurion, sporting, inappropriately, a trident decorated
with artificial grapes and a Roma football club scarf. The
soldier charges at unsuspecting passersby with a spear.

These benevolent assaults by two throwbacks from history are the publicity front for Rome's latest family attraction, Time Elevator Roma,[1] a high-tech 'joyride' back to the landmarks of Rome's history. It is the first of its kind in Europe; there's already a Time Elevator in Jerusalem and plans are afoot for Venice, Florence and Pompeii, as well as Athens, Prague and Barcelona.

The campaigning 'Roman' duo have to rely on their weapons as agents of persuasion, for their grasp of English and history is frayed beyond comprehension. The young emperor points with his dagger down a sidestreet to the entrance of the Time Elevator.

Like a new low-star hotel lobby, it is a sanitised space, decorated with imitation Roman tiles and mosaics. A plaque on the wall describes the audio-visual *spettacolo*: 'Visitors sit in dynamic simulators synchronised to the action of the film.' The ride is off-limits to children below five years of age and 100cm in height, and the sign goes on to suggest that people with back, neck and heart problems or who suffer from motion sickness may wish to sit in the stationary section. Finally, in words that wouldn't have been inappropriate on a stone tablet outside the Colosseum, it declares: 'The show includes various effects that may startle.' With the exception of the motion sickness it sounds promising.

If the show is but meta-history the building that houses Time Elevator, like almost every square inch of Rome, has its own real past. It is situated in the north side of the sixteenth-century Palazzo Odeschalchi, which once housed a studio for Bernini. In its previous incarnation it was the Majestic Cinema, which showed English language films on Monday nights. Here I'd seen such gruesome delights as *Schindler's List*, *Pulp Fiction* and *Gladiator*. Time Elevator had a lot to live up to.

I'm ushered into a room – thankfully by an unarmed girl in an ordinary uniform – for the first phase of 'edutainment', the quiz show. Contestants gather around a giant screen and try to answer multiple-choice questions about Rome by using keypad stations. The first round is in Japanese, but by the time the computer switches into English mode, I feel ready to take on the Americans in the group. Some of the questions are quite tricky; for example, you wouldn't expect every American schoolboy to know who built the Statue of Liberty let alone Ponte Sant'Angelo.

I'm slow off the mark, but then spurred on by a high-scoring competitor, I employ my unfair advantage (living in Rome). The virtual quizmaster showers me with praise: 'Congratulations, number six, that is the highest score of the day. Raise your hand.' At which point I regret the showing off and tuck the prize of last year's calendar with the dates removed into my backpack.

Next we are treated to a head-to-head between a virtual Augustus and Bernini, two men of huge influence in shaping Imperial and Baroque Rome respectively. Their virtual forms come to life on the wall behind us, among a collage of plastic Roman artefacts and dates.

For the sake of the tourists in the group, the computer discussion host poses questions in Japanese. The illuminated face of Augustus squints and frowns at the foreign language, then proceeds to explain (in modern Italian, that's then translated into Japanese and English) that he 'found Rome a city of bricks and left it as one of marble'. 'Huh,' says an animated Bernini on the adjacent wall, 'that's nothing, I endowed the city with Ponte Sant'Angelo, numerous fountains and statues . . .' A surreal duel of architectural and civic achievements ensues. Much of which goes over the heads of the Japanese still thrilled by the introductory quiz.

Before Augustus fades away he makes a plea to the bemused tourists: 'If you see Julius, warn him not to trust Brutus.' On that note of historical inaccuracy (Augustus ruled years after Julius Caesar) we enter the Time Elevator.

Thankfully the time capsules are nothing like a typical Roman lift (usually a boxy wooden affair like a vertical coffin, built at least half a century ago, that jerks to a halt between floors). We settle into rollercoaster-style pods that seat eight and are closed with a safety bar. On the four screens that wrap around the pod appears Dr Arnaldi, a zany Dr Who type, who will be our guide through the annals of Roman time. We wear headphones, and select our language.

In a little over thirty minutes as history is re-enacted on the screens, we are zoomed, jolted and shaken down through 2,753 years. We are chased by the wolves who gave suckle to the founders of Rome, Romulus and Remus; we witness the murder of Julius Caesar and a poignant, lifelike crucifixion of Christ to the strains of Mozart's Requiem; we are threatened by Nero's henchman; and berated by a pope-stifled Michelangelo on the scaffolds of the Sistine Chapel. 'Santo Dio!' exclaims our guide every time he stumbles across a seminal moment in Rome's history.

The remaining years, from the late Renaissance to present-day Rome, are covered in record time. The narrator signs off with a postcard-style flourish: 'So toss a coin into the Trevi Fountain and ensure that you'll take a trip back into the past in the near future . . . because, all roads lead to Rome.'

As I emerge from a back exit into the bright glare of the Roman sunshine, it does feel a bit like being ejected from a time machine. I take a route that avoids being speared by the pair who look like extras from *Up Pompeii* and head towards Piazza Santi Apostoli for a real-time shot of coffee.

1   TIME ELEVATOR ROMA, 20 Via dei Santi Apostoli, 06 699 0053, www.time-elevator.it, open 10am—10.30pm daily, adults €11, children aged 5 to 12 €9.20.

EXPLORA

A hands-on museum

At what seems like every junction in Rome's sprawling nexus, even when you are 30km away on the other side of the city, there is a brown signpost for the zoo. When it was renamed Bioparco a couple of years ago and given an eco-friendly facelift, the city must have gone overboard with its publicity drive. But while the Bioparco is a fun day out for kids, the city should erect more signs to Rome's true treasure for children, the urbane Explora, Il Museo dei Bambini di Roma[1] (Museum of the Children of Rome) on Via Flaminia, north of Piazza del Popolo.

Every city should have one. This private, non-profit museum was the brainchild of a group of mothers disgruntled by Rome's lack of facilities for their offspring. Housed in an award-winning, wrought-iron and glass tram-shed, and powered by solar energy, the museum is structured like a city for children.

Under-twelves can arrive at the museum and take part in workshops run by bilingual facilitators. They can learn how a letter travels (a mystery, no doubt, that all Romans would like to discover), cook a meal for their parents, perform heart surgery, print banknotes and with-draw them from a cash dispenser, read the news on live television and get to grips with recycling.

'It's where the little lords and ladies can practise being adults and get dirty which their parents don't usually allow. No doubt careers will be forged here,' Marianna Carli, one of Explora's founding mums, tells me. Carli also has plans to convert a farmhouse owned by the Torlonia family at the substantial ruins of Circus Maxentius on the Via Appia into an interactive archaeological playground for children.

The floor of the children's museum has a fascinating cut-away section showing what pipes and cables run beneath the city. The Explora architects have taken care to include a section of Roman ruins – reminding the surveyors and engineers of tomorrow of the city's all-pervasive heritage.

1   EXPLORA, IL MUSEO DEI BAMBINI DI ROMA, 80–84 Via Flaminia, 06 361 3776, www.mdbr.it, open 9.30am–5pm daily except Monday, adults €6, children €7.

KIDS' BOOKS

Bestsellers for bambini

In Piazza Santi Apostoli, which offers respite from the traffic fumes of neighbouring Piazza Venezia, is the children's bookshop Stoppani[1] (with deliciously fresh air conditioning). It stocks books in both Italian and English to whet the appetite on all the favourite subjects of Roman history, from the games at the Colosseum to military life and imperial luxury. Look out for *Ancient Rome for Kids*[2] with its blow-by-blow account of a day in the life of the Colosseum, and Caroline Lawrence's new series of mysteries set in Imperial Rome, including *The Thieves of Ostia* and *The Assassins of Rome*,[3] which make good holiday reading.

The tourist information kiosks dotted around the city offer a series of colourful leaflets that tell behind-the-scene stories about some of Rome's places most likely to appeal to young hearts and minds. But better still, an excellent shared resource for parents and kids is Fodor's *Around Rome With Kids: 68 Great Things To Do Together*[4] by Dana Prescott. Cleverly compiled and simple to read, its sight-seeing suggestions range from Castel Sant'Angelo, a beloved Roman monument with dungeons and a torture chamber, to Parco dei Mostri, a sixteenth-century sculpture garden some ninety minutes north of Rome, with grotesque statues, picnic benches and baby goats to feed. For each sight, the book recommends a nearby place to eat.

A small spiralbound guide, about the size of a large wallet, called *Rome Past and Present*[5] can be bought from bookshops and tourist stalls throughout the city. It was first published in 1962, but I still use my copy religiously today. The guide seeks to reconstruct ancient monuments and it's a great tool to spark children's imaginations. On each right-hand page there's a picture of one of Imperial Rome's principal sites, uncannily minus all human and vehicular traffic. Because the book is now over forty years old the prints have the hazy, faded look of the last-generation postcards that you still see in racks at *tabacchi* shops. But, give or take some carbon monoxide damage, the buildings remain in essentially the same ruinous state today as they did at the beginning of the 1960s.

Look closely at the 'contemporary' site, preferably in situ, and try to fire up your imagination. What would it have looked like in its mint-condition glory? Images from film and art flash across the screens of our minds, but it's difficult to build a concrete mental picture. Then, and here's the book's simple magic, by turning over a Cellophane page from the left-hand side of the book, a reconstruction is superimposed on the present-day picture. Flagstones are laid; roofs, colonnades, façades and arches are erected; and a historical link spanning 2,000 years is made. Ancient Rome arises before your very eyes.

For some buildings the changes are dramatic. The litter-ridden dustbowl that is the Circus Maximus becomes a magnificent elliptical stadium overlooked by the shiny marbled villas of Rome's elite on the Palatine hill. The three splendidly lonesome pillars that tower evocatively above the

Forum at its Capitoline end become the majestically sym-
metrical Temple of Vesta. For others, such as the Pantheon
and the Colosseum, both of which retain a strong outline of
their original forms, the second page merely obliterates
Renaissance excesses and adds adornments such as the
statues, marble and gold that were ransacked by invaders
and pious popes with building ambitions. In short, the book
is a blessing for anyone who has ever struggled to make
sense of the jumble of leftover shards and fragments of the
classical city. And, in my opinion, it's the one thing worth
buying from the stalls selling tourist tat around the city.

1   MEL GIANNINO STOPPANI, LIBRERIA PER RAGAZZI, 59/65
      Piazza Santi Apostoli, 06 6994 1045, www.melgianninostoppani.it.
2   *Ancient Rome for Kids* by Anna Parisi, Elisabetta Parisi and Rosaria Punzi,
      ed. Fratelli Palombi, €13.
3   *The Thieves of Ostia*, *The Assassins of Rome* and other mystery stories by
      Caroline Lawrence published by Orion Children's, around €8.
4   *Around Rome With Kids: 68 Great Things To Do Together* by Dana Prescott,
      Fodor, €9.
5   *Rome Past and Present* by A R Staccioli et al, Getty Trust, €20.

PUNCH AND JUDY

The wicked Pulcinella

There are two panoramic views from the top of the Janiculum hill. One is real and of Rome, an umber-brick spread of towers and domes, and the other is make-believe and depicts the handsome Bay of Naples. For, standing with your back to the view of Rome and facing the equestrian statue of Garibaldi, to the right and under the oak trees you will see Rome's smallest 'theatre' when *Cavaliere* (Sir) Carlo Pintadosi pulls back the curtains at his Punch and Judy booth. For 43 years, at weekends during the summer, he has been running a show here every bit as absorbing as any grand theatre pantomime. He is helped by his wife who sews the wooden puppets' clothes and takes the collection.

Beneath the window a sign requests that stones are not thrown and explains that the show survives thanks to the generous offerings of the public – '*Non fatelo morire – grazie*' ('Don't let it die – thank you'). A minimum of €1 is suggested.

Pintadosi is Italy's only honorary puppeteer. Officially his full title is 'Cavaliere del Lavoro', or Knight of Labour, a privilege bestowed upon him by Carlo Azeglio Ciampi, the

President of Italy, after fifty years of working as a puppeteer. 'If it wasn't already in my blood, it certainly is now,' he says about his labour of love.

Asked whether parents may not consider a husband battering his wife and tossing a baby down the stairs to be suitable entertainment for children, Pintadosi replies, 'Cast your mind back to your childhood. It's magical for children.'

Pintadosi's repertoire comprises fifteen comedies, with about as many characters, which he breaks down into twenty-minute shows. The main characters (or '*maschere*' – masks) are Pulcinella and Gabriella (better known in England as Punch and Judy), and Gabriella is the object of Pulcinella's desire. The dialogue is simple and absurd, though the nasal Neapolitan may prove tricky for beginners in Italian. When Dario, a swarthy Latin lover, tells Pulcinella that Gabriella has promised him her heart, Pulcinella retorts: 'Well, she promised me her liver and her guts.' On cue, the *bambini* writhe and squeal with laughter.

Despite her complete dissimilitude to Sophia Loren, the heroine, wearing a shapeless paisley frock and her hair in a prim bun, still manages to bewitch the male characters and the audience. It is a welcome change from the make-up-caked nymphets of prime-time Italian TV.

Pulcinella was originally a morality play, arguably based on the misfortunes of a professional comedian of that name from seventeenth-century Naples. The play even travelled to England in 1662 where it was performed at Charing Cross. The central theme is the cliché of Mezzogiorno living: '*Il dolce far niente*' ('The pleasure of doing nothing'). It's a theme still close to the hearts of many Romans. 'How Romans laugh when they see the audacious Pulcinella get away with slapping a figure of authority over the head. That's entertainment,' says Pintadosi with a chuckle.

An inscription on the booth reads '*Ridere allunga la vita – buon divertimento*' ('Laughing prolongs life – have fun'). If this is true then Pintadosi will be casting his spell on children and adults alike for many years to come.

LA BELLA FIGURA

Looking the part

Making *la bella figura* (literally, 'a beautiful figure', but in practice 'a good image') is key to the Italian way of life, and Roman children are no exception.

Rome has its own breed of young Sloane Rangers who bizarrely like to ape the dress code of the English country gentleman by dressing in Barbour jackets and brogues. These adolescents are known as 'Pariolini' from the swanky (though architecturally prosaic) Parioli neighbourhood where they live or aspire to live one day.

As well as the more usual accoutrements of Roman youth – designer clothes and the latest Nokia handset – at eighteen they will be driving the little Smart car made by Mercedes, or if younger the tiny French Micro made by Ligier which doesn't even require a driving licence. Parioli is full of these buggies which can be parked almost anywhere.

Youngsters aged fourteen to eighteen probably go to the afternoon Gilda Young disco at the sophisticated Gilda[1] nightclub on Via Mario de' Fiori, near the Spanish Steps. There are other afternoon discos in Rome but the Gilda remains *the* place for teenagers to strut their stuff. The bouncers are fiercely discerning and will not admit anyone wearing metal, hair gel, jogging bottoms or with a visible body-piercing. Not to be outdone by elder siblings and to unwind from the attentions of extended family, Gilda runs a special disco for the under-twelves, Baby Gilda, on Sunday afternoons.

Alternatively, animal-loving children might enjoy a visit to the remarkable Cat Sanctuary[2] beneath Largo di Torre Argentina. Founded in 1993 to cope with Rome's teeming strays, it is an underground cave set amid the ruins of Republican temples and filled with as many as 250 cats. The unwell are housed in neatly ordered cages while they are nursed back to health. A small sign says the sanctuary, run by volunteers, is 'committed to creating, preserving and defending the quality of life for every cat.' Certainly the cold pasta they were eating looked good enough for human consumption. Even the cats' names are chosen with great care, usually with a story behind each name.

Folklore has it that the souls of the dead reside in the cats' scrawny frames, their eyes acting as a window to antiquity. When I visited there was a Berlusconi, named after the tycoon Prime Minister who lives just down the road, and a Mussolini, Il Duce having sanctioned the excavations at the Area Sacra where the sanctuary is now based. When opening the excavations of Largo di Torre Argentina, Mussolini had said: 'I should like to have brought to me here those who opposed this work, to have them shot on the spot.' He wasn't being serious, apparently.

If you fancy a child-free night on the town and need a baby-sitter, your best bet is to go through the English Yellow Pages: look up 'Child Care' on www.intoitaly.it or phone 06 474 0861. Angels Staff Services (98 Via dei Fienili, 06 678 2877, e-mail aupairs65@hotmail.com) is a reliable organisation worth trying. Ad hoc baby-sitting is not common in Italy so you would be wise to arrange it well in advance.

1   GILDA, 97 Via Mario de' Fiori, 06 678 4838.
2   TORRE ARGENTINA CAT SANCTUARY, Largo di Torre Argentina, 06 687 2133, www.romancats.com, open noon–6pm daily.

" A thoroughly modern, cheap and eco-friendly way to see the heart of ancient Rome is to take your family on the no. 116 bus, one of the city's bright orange fleet of mini electric buses, with drivers specially trained to squeeze down alleyways jammed with parked cars and pedestrians. To ensure you get one of the eight seats, board at the *capolinea* (end of the line) opposite the Excelsior Hotel in Via Veneto, not far from the Villa Borghese. The full round-trip takes less than the ninety minutes for which your ticket is valid, so there's time to hop off by the Pantheon where some of Rome's best ice-cream shops can be found, and re-board using the same ticket. Tickets cost €0.77 and can be bought from *tabacchi* shops or newsstands. *Buon viaggio!*